Merry Christmas!
Butch
2001

Finebaum Said

First published by *The Birmingham Post Herald*,
used by permission.

Printed in the United States of America by
Vaughan Printing, Inc., Nashville Tennessee
Cover and book design by Cindy Bonds
Cover Photograph: Paul Robertson, Jr.
        NASCAR / Boat: Kent Gidley
        Big AL & Aubie: Art Meripol
        Bowl Icons: Paul Robertson, Jr.

Published by Pachyderm Press, Inc., Birmingham, Alabama.
First Edition, first printing, August 2001

ISBN 1-931656-03-7
UPC 6-42203-01101-7

Finebaum Said

by Paul Finebaum

Published by

Pachyderm Press.

100 Vestavia Parkway, Suite 300
P.O. Box 661016 (35266-1016)
Birmingham, Alabama 35216

www.pachydermpress.com

The
Paul Finebaum
Radio Network

www.finebaum.com

NETWORK AFFILIATES			
Auburn/Opelika, AL	WANI – 1400 AM	Mobile, AL	WNTM – 710 AM
Brewton, AL	WEBJ – 1240 AM	Montgomery, AL	WMSP – 740 AM
Birmingham, AL	WERC – 960 AM	Muscle Shoals, AL	WLAY – 1450 AM
Cullman, AL	WXXR – 1340 AM	Selma, AL	WMRK – 1340 AM
Decatur, AL	WHOS – 800 AM	Tallassee, AL	WTLS – 1300 AM
Gadsden, AL	WAAX – 570 AM	Tuscaloosa, AL	WACT – 1420 AM
Huntsville, AL	WBHP – 1230 AM	Chattanooga, TN	WUUS – 980 AM

Paul Finebaum is Alabama's leading sports personality and host of the state's most listened to sports-talk program – The Paul Finebaum Radio Network. Paul's pointed wit and merciless humor has gained and cultivated a vast audience that has earned the program national acclaim for it's breaking stories and in-depth interviews. Winner of THREE CONSECUTIVE Alabama Associated Press Awards for Best General Sports, the Paul Finebaum Radio Network prides itself on providing the biggest names in sports...Rick Pitino, Terry Bradshaw, Dick Vitale, Dale Earnhardt, Dick Schaap, Lee Corso, Jim Palmer and Bob Costas all have appeared on the show. Known for his aggressive yet informed approach, many of the nation's top coaches, athletes and news makers have developed a deep respect for Finebaum's style and talent. His commentaries and insight on Alabama and regional sports issues are frequently highlighted on national networks like ESPN, CNN-SI, CBS and HBO. From his acerbic approach on the day's top stories, to his tongue-in-cheek parodies, hear why more Alabamians tune into Finebaum for their dependable and credible sports-talk.

In July 2001, Paul joined *The Mobile Register* as a sports columnist. You can access his commentaries from his website at *www.finebaum.com*.

THE PAUL FINEBAUM RADIO NETWORK...
SPORTS TALK WITH AN ATTITUDE!

Table of Contents

AN 8-YEAR-OLD'S ADORATION FOR JORDAN MORE THAN IDLE WORSHIP

June 11, 1994

Michael Jordan's baseball career might be a flop. The critics might be urging him to go back to basketball. But, to some people, he still is the greatest of them all. Who says? Eight-year old Ben Gold, that's who. Ben is my nephew ("and I'll be 9 on June 20, Uncle Paul, so don't forget").

He's also the biggest Michael Jordan fan in the world. Well, that is, on days when he's not the biggest Charles Barkley fan in the world. That is, on days when he's not the biggest Anfernee Hardaway fan in the world.

Well, Ben, who lives in Memphis, visited Birmingham the other day. Naturally, it wasn't long before the car was pointed toward the Hoover Met.

"How long do you think we'll be able to talk to Michael?" Ben said on the drive to Hoover.

I tried to explain to Ben that although my position as a sportswriter often can open doors (as well as have some slammed in my face) in gaining access to well-known people, it probably doesn't mean diddly to the most famous athlete in the world.

"Well, I'll just tell him you are Charles Barkley's best friend," Ben quipped.

I began to explain to Ben that while I was friendly with Sir Charles, Michael actually is his best friend. But I decided against that. Ben might be 9 in two weeks, but some things are better left unsaid.

My hope was to get to the game midway through and stick around a short time afterward, with the hopes of getting an autograph. But a one-hour, 19-minute rain delay put a halt to that.

But Ben was ready, nevertheless.

He wore a Phoenix Suns No. 34 jersey with Barkley's name on the back. He had Air Charles (Barkley) Nike shoes on his feet. He also wore his Chicago Bulls warm-up jacket and a Charlotte Hornets hat that would have made Alexander Julian proud.

"Do you think I ought to wear the Charlotte Hornets hat?" he said.

"Why not?" I said.

"Well, you know Jordan's father got killed in North Carolina," the 8 year-old responded.

When we got to the game, it was about to start, and Michael was in right field playing catch with a pitcher. Naturally, Ben ran over to the wall and began screaming, "Michael ... Michael."

For the next hour or so, we meandered around the ballpark, going from souvenir stand to concession stand (any place that had products with a price tag).

Finally, the big moment arrived in the bottom of the second inning. Mighty Michael came out of the dugout to take his place on the on-deck circle.

Ben ran to the backstop behind home plate, so he could get close to his idol. He tried to get his attention a couple of times.

Once or twice, Michael looked toward Ben. The second time, he appeared, for just a glancing moment, to be winking.

Michael dribbled a pathetic grounder to second base and reached first when the infielder missed the tag on the runner. When he made it around to home, Ben began cheering even louder.

"Go Michael," he said. "Go Barons."

After that, his interest in the game and getting Michael's autograph quelled.

First, Jim Dunaway, a sports reporter for Channel 13, had asked Ben to yell, "Go Barons!" to start that night's highlights package of the game. Ben seemed more interested in going home to watch himself on television than in waiting until 11:30 p.m. to see Michael after the game.

Finebaum Said...

For once, I had to admit that television sportscasters had some worth. The ride home was interesting.

"I hope Michael isn't mad at me for talking badly about him," Ben said. "I mean, I didn't mean to say earlier that he was a bad baseball player. I just meant that he is the big enchilada in basketball. He is the greatest basketball player ever. But in baseball, he just isn't very good."

I tried to explain that Michael probably wasn't mad.

"Did you see him wink at me?" Ben said. "I think he knows what a big fan I am."

But Ben was still bothered by his earlier criticism (he definitely takes after his Uncle Paul in that category) of Michael, that he should give up baseball and go back to the game where he belongs.

"He has to be pretty good, though," Ben said. "I mean, he couldn't have made the Barons if he wasn't. And he couldn't have gotten on base and made it to home plate tonight."

I started to explain to Ben about the name and fame that Jordan brings to a game.

I started to tell him that anyone else batting .199 would be playing in the Cuban league for free cigars instead of in a multi-million dollar ballpark in Hoover and riding a luxury bus when he wasn't jetting to and from charity golf tournaments.

But Ben wasn't listening anyway.

In the black of the still summer night, Ben was talking incessantly about his visit to the Hoover Met and his close encounter with Michael Jordan.

"That was the most fun I ever had," Ben said. "This has been the greatest day of my whole life, ever."

LUMPKIN WAS A SPORTSWRITER'S SPORTSWRITER

July 4, 1994

Unfortunately, the concluding years of a sportswriter often are filled with disillusion and frustration. There is burnout and a sense of lassitude, a time of wonderment about the past and the future. Interestingly, Bill Lumpkin's final year as sports editor of the *Birmingham Post Herald* might have been his best. His writing was crisp and provocative. And his public image was never higher, as he appeared frequently on local television and radio shows. He was elected to the Alabama Sports Writers Association Hall of Fame. Yet, perhaps the biggest part of Lumpkin's final year was his role as president of the Football Writers Association of America. For a period in December, Lumpkin seemingly was on a plane every other day, flying from awards ceremony to awards ceremony, often appearing on national television.

His many appearances brought great recognition to the newspaper for which he worked for 38 years and was a fitting tribute to one of the finest sportswriters of this region.

I came into this business 15 years ago and, like many other young scions of the post-Watergate era, thought I was going to change the world. I had disdain for anyone older than 30 in the newspaper business, and for a short time that included Bill Lumpkin.

But as I spent more time around Lumpkin, I discovered he was different. Unlike many sportswriters of his day, he was more interested in searching for the truth than in hiding it.

Certainly, he was friendly with the major figures of the day, people such as Ralph Jordan and Paul Bryant. But when there was a big story to tackle, Lumpkin never thought twice about diving in head first.

Finebaum Said...

That was never more evident than in the summer of 1981. Rubin Grant and I had broken a monumental story on Bobby Lee Hurt, the Huntsville basketball star who had ended a controversial recruiting war by signing with Alabama. Several accusations were leveled in the story toward the University of Alabama basketball program and Coach Wimp Sanderson. The NCAA looked into the matter, but it never opened a formal investigation.

However, Lumpkin began hearing rumblings that there was more to the story. By midsummer, the *Post-Herald*, with Lumpkin firmly on board, broke a major story, alleging that money was given to Hurt from the high school principal at Butler High School from soft-drink machines so he would not transfer to another school. The stories also reported that money from home basketball game receipts was used to pay for an expensive dental bill for Hurt.

I spent most of that summer in Huntsville with Lumpkin. His age and experience was critical. While law enforcement and local officials were likely to throw me out of their office (I was 23 years old and had a beard), they would talk to Lumpkin, whom they knew and respected.

The high school principal sued the *Post Herald* for $6.9 million. Even the judge during the case, who seemed to go out of his way to castigate the *Post Herald's* team of lawyers, often would joke with Lumpkin. The two had known each other for years.

Some trial veterans believed Lumpkin's testimony was a key in the *Post Herald* winning the libel case, which was heralded as a landmark ruling for newspapers.

One of the pivotal moments of the trial occurred when defense counsel Warren Lightfoot of Birmingham asked Lumpkin if he believed the story when he wrote it.

Lumpkin paused, slowly took his glasses off and held them in his hands, then said: "If I didn't believe it, I wouldn't have written it. I believed it then, I believed it yesterday and I'll believe it tomorrow."

The jury returned several days later and ruled in favor of the *Post-Herald*.

While that was one of the great moments Lumpkin and I shared, one of the darker ones came two years earlier.

I had been at the *Post Herald* for a short time when rumors began to surface about the possible firing of Auburn football coach Doug Barfield. Lumpkin was all over the story, boldly stating in his column five weeks before the season ended that Barfield and Lee Hayley, the embattled athletic director, were on their way out.

After the final game against Alabama, the rumors began swirling that Georgia coach Vince Dooley was on his way back to Auburn.

It was believed that then Gov. Fob James, Dooley's former Auburn roommate, was the driving force.

Yep, that's the same old Fob now running again.

On the Sunday after the game, I was working on a speculative story, saying that Dooley had emerged as the leading candidate. Still, there was no confirmation. Just a lot of scuttlebutt.

At approximately 11:10 p.m., almost the time the story was being set to go to press, the phone rang. It was Lumpkin. "Paul, it's Bill," the voice on the phone said.

"It's Dooley."

What? I couldn't believe the matter-of-fact tone in Lumpkin's voice.

Lumpkin told me to go ahead and write it up, saying Dooley will be named the coach. It was a done deal, so to speak.

The story, at Lumpkin's exhortation, was copyrighted and spread across six columns of the front page, under the headline: "Dooley to be Auburn Coach." After reading the story back to Lumpkin, I asked: "Bill, should I just put your byline on the story?"

Although I had done much of the work, it was Bill's story and he was the sports editor.

Bill paused, then said: "No, Paul, just go ahead and put yours on there."

For some reason, I put both of ours.

When the story appeared a few hours later, the Georgia administration became mad and was able to keep Dooley at Georgia.

"I had seen the actual press release from Auburn which had the Dooley announcement," Lumpkin said.

We were ridiculed by many of our brethren, as well as the public at large. But we also broke the story two days later that Dooley was staying at Georgia.

Many people believed afterward that if that story had not come out, Auburn officials probably would have signed Dooley behind the scenes.

What always has impressed me so much was how well Lumpkin was known and the amount of respect he had earned throughout a lifetime in sportswriting. That never was more apparent to me than in September 1988, when Lumpkin and I flew to College Station, Texas, for the Alabama-Texas A&M game.

For days, there was speculation the game would be called off because of the threat of Hurricane Gilbert hitting Texas. But the decision to play the game was made. However, as we checked in at the hotel, we were stunned to learn the game had been called off.

Suddenly, we were faced with an incredibly important breaking story. So Lumpkin and I jumped in our rental car and drove to the athletic department, with the hope of talking to Jackie Sherrill, head coach and athletic director at Texas A&M.

Lumpkin assured me we could get to see Sherrill. But after looking around and seeing teams of television camera operators and other reporters, I had serious doubts.

However, as we waited in the antechamber, who should appear but Sherrill.

"Lump!" Sherrill said. "What are you doing here?"

He immediately ushered us into his office where we chatted for about an hour.

Now that we (actually, Lumpkin) had talked to him, we

needed to get back and write our story. But that wasn't the end of it for Sherrill.

"What are you guys doing for dinner?" he asked.

Sherrill picked us up and we dined along with his wife at one of College Station's finest culinary delights.

The next morning, Lumpkin convinced Sherrill to be a guest on my Birmingham radio show. Afterward, we met him at local sports bar and spent the next four hours eating, drinking, watching college football and trashing Bill Curry (and not necessarily in that order).

After that weekend, I never doubted Lumpkin's influence in the sports world.

Lumpkin used to spend hours fishing at Pat Dye's farm near Reeltown. They would joke and laugh and talk as if they were brothers. Three days later, Lumpkin might be carving Dye's play-calling to shreds in his *Post Herald* column.

Lumpkin could criticize Curry about any number of issues. But Curry still would talk to Bill and even return his phone calls.

The same goes for Gene Stallings.

People have respected Lumpkin for many reasons. I have always thought the main reason was that Lumpkin never tried to be anything but a good newspaper man. That was his love and he did it with aplomb.

However, I am disappointed with Lumpkin's decision to retire. Partly because he is one of my closest friends at the newspaper. He has always been there to commiserate with me in times of trouble. But more important, I still think Lumpkin has important things to say and I hope he'll consider writing a periodic column.

Just last Friday, as Lumpkin was cleaning out his desk after four decades at the *Post Herald*, there was a letter to the editor blasting him for a recent column on O.J. Simpson. Even at the end, Lumpkin was doing his job: getting people to think and react to a newspaper column.

However, I don't blame him for wanting to take it easy. He

has a devoted wife and four kids and grandchildren to babysit.

It is hard to do all of that while listening to Alabama fans bellyache that he is prejudiced toward Auburn. It is difficult to do that while tracking down continual rumors about another major scandal on the local sports scene.

So I don't fault Bill for stepping back and taking a deep breath, for walking through life at a slightly slower pace.

But I am going to miss him terribly. I will miss seeing him at the newspaper and miss reading his column. I'll miss him chomping one peanut after another at Alabama and Auburn games and joining in with me as we criticize Stallings and Terry Bowden for dumb play-calling.

It just won't be the same. Though Lumpkin might be slowing his pace, he has left us with a lifetime of memories to cherish. And for that, we are all very thankful.

HIS FRIEND VINCE SEZ... My Friend Vince Sez and Bill Lumpkin have had a fast friendship that goes back to the mid-1960s, when Vince distributed bird seed and other pet products for Hartz.

He made Lumpkin's "Hanging Out the Wash" Tuesday column famous. Readers often told Lumpkin they read the bottom of the column first because that's where "My Friend Vince Sez" closed it with a clever saying.

Readers also want to know if Vince is real. Yes, he is. He's Vince Saia, president of Rams, Inc., a brokerage firm for perishable food. His brother, Claude Saia, is a former Auburn assistant football coach under Ralph "Shug" Jordan. We can't tell you the exact date "My Friend Vince" debuted in "Hanging Out the Wash." We think it was in late 1969.

Since then, My Friend Vince Sez became a fixture. His sayings have made *Reader's Digest*, been picked up in note columns in a New York newspaper and carried in syndication by many Scripps Howard newspapers. He has become more famous than the columnist.

So, as Lumpkin enters into retirement, he presents a few of the best of My Friend Vince Sez, which have appeared in the wash column over the years: The best way to get back on your feet is to miss two car payments... His boss gave each employee as a Christmas gift a 114-piece after-dinner set. A box of toothpicks... There was this secretary whose typing improved so much that she gave up tight sweaters... You're getting older when the girl you smile at thinks you're one of her dad's friends... A friend and his date froze to death at the movies. They went to see "Closed For The Winter" at a drive-in... On his secretary's desk was a sign that read: "I type the way I live - fast, with a lot of mistakes"... He defines an optimist as a fellow who thinks the cleaners are shrinking his pants. He defines a sad case as 24 empties... His bartender has come up with a new football cocktail. You're lucky if you get the first down... A bachelor is like detergent: works fast and leaves no ring... He defines a psychologist as a guy who, when a beautiful girl enters the room, watches everybody else... The best way to raise vegetables is with a fork... The best way to double your money is to fold it... The best get well card is a third ace... Money isn't everything, but it sure does keep a man in touch with the kids... He tells friends who complain about not meeting any new people that all they have to do is pick up the wrong golf ball... He bought some perfume for his wife that is so powerful that it has been banned by Planned Parenthood... Poise is the ability to talk fluently while the other fellow pays the check... The trick is to have a good day. Any fool can have a good night... Thanks to jogging, more people than ever before are collapsing in perfect health... If the meek inherit the Earth, they will inherit enough debt to keep them that way... Just about the time he catches up with the Joneses, they go and get refinanced... Hair and money only seem important when you no longer have either... People who snore always fall asleep first... The best proof that appearances are deceiving is the fact the dollar bill looks exactly the same as it did

Finebaum Said...

15 years ago...What's 10, 9, 8, 7, 6...? It's Bo Derek growing old...
Card playing can be expensive, but so can any game where you
begin by holding hands...Many people aren't really eager to learn
the secret of success, because they've heard rumors it's hard
work...A tip on how to tell when you're getting old is when, after
painting the town red, you have to take a long rest before apply-
ing the second coat...Eating fish might not nourish the brain, but
trying to catch them certainly strengthens the imagination...If you
want to write something that will last forever, sign a mortgage...
Only kisses and money could be so full of germs and still be so
popular...Women live longer than men because they need the extra
time to finish what they were saying...A hospital bed these days is
the closest thing to a parked taxi with the meter running...Paying
alimony is like having the TV set on after you've fallen asleep...
When he got his bill for surgery, he found out why doctors wear
masks in the operating room...The sex of the young is determined
by genes and obscured by jeans...He knows a guy who read so
much about the evils of drink that he gave up reading...An optimistic gardener is a person who believes what goes down must
come up...The good thing about a conscience is that it never both-
ers you until the fun is over...Middle age is when you get out of the
shower and are glad the mirror's fogged up...When Eli Whitney
declared proudly, "I've invented the cotton gin," his wife grumbled
and replied: "Who needs a fluffy martini?"

Please, don't ask where My Friend Vince Sez comes up with
all these witty gems. He's sworn to secrecy.

BARKER SETS HIGH STANDARD FOR OTHERS

October 5, 1994

In Alabama, it is often said that football is like a religion and Saturday is the high holy day. That often extends to early Sunday morning, especially after a heart-stopping victory such as Alabama's 29-28 victory over Georgia. But Sunday morning, at Briarwood Presbyterian Church -one of the state's largest places of worship- the topic of conversation was not about winners and losers.

According to Tom Caradine, the associate pastor, "The topic of conversation was "Did you hear Jay's comments on ESPN?""

Jay, of course, is Jay Barker, the senior quarterback, who not only played his best game at Alabama, but perhaps played one of the greatest games of any quarterback in the school's storied football history.

What he said on ESPN was not the usual football babble. Amid screaming fans in a frenzied stadium, Barker was asked to comment on his stellar performance (396 yards and two touchdowns on 26-of-34 passing).

Barker told the ESPN commentator:

"First of all, right now, I want to thank my Lord, Jesus Christ. There has been so much criticism, but the Lord says in the Bible, 'Humble yourselves, therefore, under the mighty hand of God, that he may exalt you at the proper time.'"

The verse comes from I Peter 5:6. Some people might take exception to such comments, saying a football game is not the appropriate place to discuss one's faith.

But listening to Barker, one was struck by what a wonderful example and role model he is to the rest of the nation.

Here is Jay Barker, in a state assailed by the nation's media for Wedowee and Shoal Creek, saying things that might help a young man or woman out there in the hinterlands get his or her life on the right path. It was especially significant coming two weeks to the night after another Birmingham-area native, Heather Whitestone, was speaking about her faith and the challenges she has overcome before winning the Miss America Pageant on national television.

There were many things that had to be running through Barker's mind at that particular moment. But for a young man to have the presence of mind to say what he did has struck a chord with people around the nation.

Of course, if anyone is surprised by Barker's comments, they have not been paying close attention to his story.

What you see with Barker is what you get.

Caradine said Barker was invited this past summer to Briarwood to speak at the Student Stampede Youth Ministry for high school students. Approximately 300 teenagers attended.

"Jay's topic was personal success," Caradine said. "He measures success in doing what he perceives to be the will of God for his life. It was in that context, he said, 'I am eight days from my 22nd birthday and haven't drank or smoked, taken drugs and I'm still a virgin.'"

Caradine defended Barker's right to share God's message after the game, saying, "Here is a young man who sincerely in his heart is trying to live the Christian life and bringing glory to his God and not himself. In this free country, why does he not have the right to express that if it is in his heart?" It is a good question posed by the pastor, although there has been and will continue to be criticism of athletes who mention their faith in interviews and who pray before a big play.

Does God really care who wins a sporting event?

"God can use either victory or defeat in the life of a Christian athlete to bring himself glory," Caradine said. "There are Christians on both teams and God, in my opinion, is using both to bring himself glory." Some people might wish to argue these issues. But there is no argument over the standard Jay Barker has set for the rest of the nation.

BOSWELL BRINGS JOY TO ALL WHO KNOW HIM

March 29, 1995

Since Charley Boswell was rushed to the hospital last week after a fall, the phone calls to family members have poured in not only from the area but from across the globe. One of the first calls came from Palm Springs, CA. "It was Bob Hope," said Steve Boswell, one of Charley's sons. "He had heard about Dad and just wanted to check in."

Boswell and Hope are the best of friends. Boswell and his wife, Kitty, were scheduled to go to California later this spring to spend a few days at Hope's home.

Hope and his wife, Delores, did the same with the Boswells a few years ago when he was here to play in the Bruno's Memorial Classic.

Other notables have called as well, including CBS golf broadcaster Ken Venturi, another pal of Boswell's. But Boswell's illness has touched tens of thousands of people whom he never has met.

Frankly, in Charley Boswell's world, there is no such thing as a stranger.

The phone at Boswell's insurance agency has been ringing off the hook because of folks who are trying to find out his condition.

The 78-year-old Boswell just has that effect on people.

My wife met Boswell a couple of years ago for the first time. A few months later, we saw Boswell at a function. Boswell not only remembered her name but immediately recognized her voice. This from having met her one time.

His trademark salutation for friends is "Good to see you again."

This coming from a man who has been blind since a shell exploded near him while he was trying to save someone else during World War II.

Raymond Payne, who is Boswell's driver, said the past few days have been difficult. However, Payne said he is hopeful of Boswell's recovery.

"I think he is going to come through this," Payne said. "He moved his leg the other day and even stuck his tongue out at one of the doctors."

Payne said he was encouraged Monday when doctors at HealthSouth Medical Center upgraded his condition from critical to serious.

Until last week, Boswell was in great health. He still worked and practiced golf when he could.

Meanwhile, Payne would drive him across town, visiting with his legions of friends. Asked exactly what he does for Boswell, Payne said: "I drive him around and love him to death."

There really isn't another feeling one can have about Boswell after getting to know him.

He is perhaps the most charming, loving man I have met. Though he remains loyal to his beloved Alabama, Boswell is not shy when expressing an opinion about a coaching decision or the performance of a player.

He doesn't mind sharing a comment about the opinion of a certain newspaper columnist, either. Often he has gone through one of my columns verbatim. The newspaper is read to Boswell daily.

But that is Charley.

He is never one to shy away from anything, which is why his many friends are hopeful of his recovery.

Finebaum Said...

Because of Boswell's charisma, one often forgets about his blindness. About two years ago, I sat next to him at a Super Bowl party.

Because there was a large crowd chatting, Boswell couldn't hear the sound from the television well. So he began to ask me to describe the action.

For the next hour, I took over from Dick Enberg as the play-by-play announcer.

Finally, I looked to Charley and said jokingly, "Charley, you're wearing me out!"

He just smiled that famous toothy grin and asked me to get him another drink.

While Boswell has met practically every major sports celebrity of the past six decades, his favorite subject is Bob Hope.

Hope and Boswell always enjoyed a small wager when they played golf together.

Once, in front of a fairly large crowd, the two were bantering back and forth about an upcoming golf game. Hope named the game and wager.

"But I want to name the place and time," Boswell said.

"No problem," Hope said. "My course at midnight," Boswell said.

It was Boswell who had the most famous comedian in the world in stitches.

But that is Charley Boswell. And here's hoping he'll be around a long time to crack jokes on Bob Hope and bring joy to all the lives that he touches.

BO WILL KNOW SUCCESS WHEREVER LIFE TAKES HIM

April 4, 1995

Bo knows retirement. Say it ain't so.

Unfortunately, it's over for Bo.

Arguably the greatest athlete in the history of Alabama and one of the finest to play any game, Jackson officially announced his retirement from professional sports yesterday.

It came with little fanfare. There were no press conferences carried live on CNN and ESPN.

Instead, Vincent "Bo" Jackson announced his retirement in an interview with *USA Today*.

It was not a surprise.

Jackson's football career was ended prematurely because of a hip injury. While he continued to play major league baseball, his career had become impertinent. The 32-year-old Jackson simply figured it was better to end now than to hang on like so many others before him. And who could really blame him for not wanting to play major league baseball anymore?

Of course, Jackson won't exactly be disappearing from the scene altogether. He made his television debut last week as a nanny in "Diagnosis Murder."

Jackson has signed with the William Morris Agency, and one would expect him to appear in more TV and movie roles. He also is involved deeply with HealthSouth CEO Richard Scrushy as the head of the HealthSouth Sports Medicine Council.

Jackson told *USA Today* one of his goals is to be remembered as more than a jock. "When I leave this world, I want people to say, "He was a good athlete. But he was a great businessman.'"

It is difficult to put in proper words what a truly magnificent athlete Jackson was in his prime. Not only was he a skilled runner, he became a genius marketer.

Jackson's decision to play baseball in 1986 instead of professional football -that, after being the No. 1 player taken in the NFL draft- stunned the sports world.

All people could talk about was Bo.

Briefly, Bo was bigger than Michael.

His Nike commercials became landmark advertisements for the industry. But Jackson would shock the sports world again when he decided to play professional football. His career with the LA Raiders ended prematurely in 1991. Everyone figured Bo's career was finished.

But the will and determination of this man from McCalla lived on. He thrived on fooling the experts.

Jackson would play baseball again. While he never was quite the same, Jackson made a good living.

On a personal level, it always has been difficult to embrace Jackson. He could be surly and arrogant. While Phoenix Suns star Charles Barkley often returned home to Birmingham and was visible, Jackson's appearances were rare at the zenith of his career.

People who worked with him on various projects said he was difficult. The same people said Barkley was charming.

But Jackson didn't care. He made his mark. He was sure of his place in history. He was devoted to his family. Jackson said this week his family had an impact on his final decision. It bothered him recently when his 6-year-old son asked his mother why his father was never home, and wondered if he had another family.

"If that isn't enough for any man to make up his mind, then he isn't a man," Jackson said, "and he isn't a father."

So he is gone now, but he never will be forgotten.

It is unlikely Jackson's numbers will get him in either the Baseball or Pro Football Hall of Fame.

But it shouldn't be long before he finds a place in the College Football Hall of Fame and, of course, the Alabama Sports Hall of Fame.

Perhaps Jackson someday will come back home and make a difference.

It seems like yesterday he was running wild for McAdory High School. It seems like such a short time ago he was spurning Bear Bryant for Pat Dye.

It seems like yesterday when some numb-skull ranked him as only the fourth best college football prospect in the state of Alabama.

We never will see Bo Jackson on an athletic field. But he never, ever will be forgotten.

It is unclear what Jackson will be doing from here on.

But one has the feeling he will be a success.

That is one thing Bo knows a lot about.

AUGUSTA NATIONAL
A RACE AGAINST TIME?

April 6, 1995

AUGUSTA, Ga. – The primary color every year at Augusta National is green. And there are many shades of it.

From the emerald fairways and greens to the slightly lighter color of the coveted green jacket to the tint of money that is omnipresent at every step of this famed piece of real estate.

But this year, a darker color is getting the attention. The reason is Eldrick "Tiger" Woods, who today will become only the fourth black man to compete in the most prestigious golf tournament in the land.

Of course, that should not come as a surprise.

Since winning the 1994 U.S. Amateur Championship, Woods' pilgrimage to Augusta has been chronicled on practically every sports page in the universe. The presence of a black golfer on these hallowed grounds has stirred much conversation, but so far, little controversy.

It is unclear how Woods will finish in this year's Masters. But it is unlikely the attention paid to his race will affect his performance.

Still, it is difficult -and painful- for many people to reflect on the history of this club and not see racism.

Many people remember 1968, when Lee Elder became the first black man to compete in the Masters.

It was a milestone event because so much had been made out of the denial of an invitation to Charlie Sifford, who many people believed had earned one earlier with several significant tour victories during the '60s.

Sifford never has stopped blasting the tournament, saying "it was the worst redneck tournament in the country run by people who openly discriminate against blacks."

Perhaps Sifford was right at the time. But this club, and the world of golf, has changed dramatically since then.

Following the Shoal Creek controversy in 1990, Augusta National admitted its first black member. The story made the front page of *The New York Times*.

Recently, a second black member, Bill Simms (a minority owner of the Carolina Panthers), was admitted. It went unnoticed and without fanfare.

Augusta National now has a better and clearer understanding of its past. Under the leadership of Chairman Jack Stephens, it is determined to move forward into the 21st century.

In 1968, when Augusta officials welcomed Elder, it was a peculiar sight. They were courteous. However, it seemed as if the chairman at the time was shaking hands with Elder with one hand while using the other to hold his nose.

This week, the antithesis has been true.

Some people at Augusta National almost have fallen over

themselves trying to help Woods become better acquainted with the golf course and the setting.

But it has not stopped the criticism of the club.

An HBO special the other night labeled Augusta National as "The American Singapore."

Frank Deford, the former *Sports Illustrated* editor who did the piece, went on to say, "Small and rich, efficient and successful, spotless and humorless and totally unforgiving."

Deford said the club represents "the last dictatorship in sports... cold and sanctimonious, even selfish, giving little back to its game or to its community."

With all due respect to Mr. Deford (who has been on most Alabamians' drop-dead list since a 1981 profile of Bear Bryant that described intermittent pit stops on the highway between Birmingham and Tuscaloosa), I believe he has the wrong sport in mind. He could have been describing major-league baseball.

Augusta National is run like a dictatorship, but let's not forget that it is a private club and not a public entity.

The selfish claim comes from the fact that Augusta National -unlike other events such as the Bruno's Memorial Classic- doesn't give proceeds to charities. The money made off the Masters is pumped back into the golf course to make it appear as the most fantastic place on Earth for four days every April.

But for all the things that are wrong about Augusta, there are many more things right. There is no event quite like this golf tournament, be it the Super Bowl, the World Series (that is, when it is played) or the Final Four.

There is an ambience about the Masters that is special and different because of one significant reason: tradition. Time moves slowly at Augusta National. But it is wrong to say this tournament is out of touch with society.

Some things do change. Even some antediluvian attitudes about society.

Jack Nicklaus, who has won six Masters championships and

arguably is the greatest golfer of all time, had large galleries following him this week. So did Greg Norman and Fred Couples and
Nick Faldo.

But the person drawing the biggest crowds and the most
attention has been Tiger Woods.

He might only be the fourth black to play at Augusta
National in 61 years. But today, he is the most riveting competitor
at Augusta National and hopefully will be for many years to come.

IT'S WRONG FOR COX INCIDENT TO JUST FADE AWAY

April 10, 1995

As the shocking details surfaced last summer about the violent
relationship between O.J. and Nicole Brown Simpson, many people wondered how problems like that could have gone unnoticed.

Not only friends of the couple, but the local judicial system
allowed them to push the problems under the rug. Now, Nicole
Brown Simpson is dead and everybody acts surprised.

One can only hope that Pamela Cox doesn't end up the
same way.

One can only hope the Atlanta Braves organization doesn't
look the other way if there are serious -and potentially dangerous-
problems brewing at the home of Pamela and Bobby Cox, the
highly successful skipper of the baseball team.

Perhaps we are peeking through bedroom windows making
such statements. However, if anyone believes the charade that
took place at Atlanta-Fulton County Stadium on Monday, they are
plain stupid.

Some of the statements probably sent the psychiatric community going through the roof.

About the confrontation, Cox said: "It was just a domestic dispute that has brewing a little bit for the last five, six months, I guess. I'm probably not paying enough attention to what's going on at home."

Now, this guy is a real inspiration to equal-partner marriage.

Cox acts as if he really has been busy the last months. In case anyone forgot, baseball was dark from last August until this spring. But Cox didn't have time to concentrate on his home life.

About the allegations he punched his wife, Cox said: "There was no hitting of any sort. I grabbed her forehead and her hair a little bit just to keep her at a distance away from me. But she was - we both were going at it pretty good."

Apparently Cox has been watching his team so much this season he doesn't realize what hitting is. Since when does grabbing your wife by the forehead and pulling her hair not qualify as violence?

Were they just play-acting a scene from the next WWF undercard on TBS?

Of course, Pam Cox's comments are more laughable and perhaps tragic. She acted like it was no big deal. Just a minor argument that has been brewing for six months and, by the way, she just wanted him to leave the house.

However, the night before, in the official police report, Pam Cox told police that incidents like this have occurred often and that she never called police because of possible media attention and the effect it might have on her children.

She also said her husband referred to her as "a bitch."

She did the right thing by calling the police. But her quick recantation might prove costly in the end.

The Atlanta Braves have done their best to put the most positive spin on the story. One can bet this franchise, one of the most precious in baseball, wanted to end this controversy as quickly as possible. With huge television ratings at stake, they don't want women's groups labeling their beloved manager as a wife-beater.

So they arranged a quick little news conference to end this saga before it has a chance to get a life of its own.

John Schuerholz, the Braves general manager, laughed it off like an overdue parking ticket.

"I'm not an interrogator; that's not my job."

That sounds like the attitude displayed by Alabama Athletic Director Hootie Ingram the first time he heard of trouble between basketball coach Wimp Sanderson and his secretary.

Perhaps the correct thing for Schuerholz to do would have been to give Cox time off so he could have that long overdue chat with his wife. But because she claimed it was no big deal, why bother? After all, the Braves were mired in a terrible losing streak and baseball attendance is on the wane.

The Braves' attendance has been awful this year for a club that was one of the hottest draws in baseball the past couple of years. Monday night, hours after the masquerade party with Pamela and Bobby Cox, the Braves drew a crowd of 27,000.

So what happens from here?

Bobby Cox continues to manage while the Braves and the city of Atlanta look the other way.

Meanwhile, Pamela Cox gets to remain married to one of the most famous men in Atlanta.

Just a wonderful life, huh?

Nicole Brown Simpson once had the same lifestyle until a knife got in the way of her happiness.

A TOAST TO MANTLE?
LOOK AGAIN

June 10, 1995

My brethren in the news media are at it again. Everyone is pouring sugar and spice and everything nice on their computer keys and writing syrupy prose about Mickey Mantle. His story is sad and tragic, and one would have to be like Mephistopheles not to feel bad for this fallen man. Personally, I am outraged at Mantle's life and what he did to himself. Like many youngsters of my generation, Mickey Mantle was my first hero.

As a kid, when I wouldn't eat my green beans and carrots, my parents would say, "If you want to grow up and be like Mickey Mantle, you'd better eat them all up."

I ate them because I wanted to be like Mick. As his career faded, my interests naturally turned to other athletes. The more I heard and read about Mantle, the sorrier I was that I ate those vegetables. I really didn't want to be like Mickey, after all.

I didn't want to grow up to close down every bar in town. I didn't want to embarrass my family (at least, because of drinking). I didn't want to spend my life a slobbering drunk.

A friend of Mantle's called me the other day and maintained it is unfair to call him a "drunk."

"I played against Mantle for many years, and I never saw him drunk at a game," said Norm Zauchin, a local man who played big league ball with the Boston Red Sox and Washington Senators.

"Now, everybody drank a few beers after the game. We played in the daytime back then, and the club encouraged us to have a couple of beers just to get fluids back in the body."

"But it would be wrong to call Mickey Mantle a drunk."

There is no question Mickey Mantle was a sweetheart of a guy. When he wasn't drinking, Mantle always was trying to help somebody. He was involved in countless charities.

Mantle was a hero to many.

But does Mantle deserve the adulation the world currently is bestowing upon him?

Is Magic Johnson a hero because he has AIDS? Is O.J. Simpson a fallen hero because he was charged with killing his wife?

Who will be next on the fallen hero hit parade?

In each of these three cases, the result should not have surprised anyone - although the news media has fallen over backward when each of the three men has fallen. Anyone who knew the private antics of Magic Johnson could have predicted trouble for the basketball giant. O.J. Simpson's friends were acutely aware of the running back's tormented relationship with his former wife.

Mantle has been on a collision course with liver cancer since he took his first drink as a teenager.

Some people think he had a reason.

Mantle's father died of Hodgkin's disease when he was 39. His grandfather and two of his uncles were felled by the disease as well. Perhaps Mantle figured he was going young, so why not go out swinging?

Mantle has said he began drinking after his father's death to cope with it. Who really knows why we do such things?

My father died when I was 15, but I didn't head for the nearest bar. I simply tried to make something out of my life.

Drinking was Mickey Mantle's escape from reality. But the drinking also sent his life reeling back to reality from the fantasy world created by the binges.

One of the many tragedies of the Mantle story, is that so many people looked away. While Mantle was making a spectacle of himself as a slobbering drunk, his buddies simply ordered another round.

One must applaud Mantle for finally coming to grips last year with his illness, for attempting to do something about it.

Of course, his doctor warned him his next drink would be

his last.

But one cannot applaud Mantle's legions of fans who never tried to stop him.

Of course, ultimately, we are responsible for our own lives. Mantle and Billy Martin, his old drinking buddy with the Yankees, used to have a running gag.

"Billy and I used to kid each other," Mantle often said, "about whose liver would give out first."

Martin died several years ago in a car accident, the result of what else but too much drinking. Mantle is holding on for dear life today in a Dallas hospital for much the same reason.

Some sportswriter or broadcaster will say today or tomorrow or sometime soon that hopefully others can learn from Mantle's foibles.

Somehow, that will make Mantle's mistakes seem better. That will allow us to cope better with the cataclysmic decline of an American hero.

But don't believe it.

We have heard this song and dance too often before. It's only an excuse to help lessen the sting. Perhaps this sounds obdurate at a time like this.

But Mickey Mantle has no one to blame now but Mickey Mantle.

PERHAPS ALABAMA'S FINALLY PAYING FOR HAUGHTY ATTITUDE

August 3, 1995

Not since Bear Bryant's death has the Alabama family experienced such shock and hurt. But yesterday, at every turn, Alabama faithful shook their heads and wondered what went wrong.

It was as if Hurricane Erin took a wrong turn and ravaged Tuscaloosa and the Alabama football program in its path.

So what went wrong? Even during the final moments of the University of Alabama's 982-day odyssey, better known as the NCAA investigation, officials at the school did not seem to have a clue.

Some still were saying this entire episode was much ado about nothing.

For that reason, perhaps some can find equity in the NCAA's staggering decision yesterday to ban the Tide from postseason bowl appearances in 1995, strip them of additional scholarships and just about break their spirit. Perhaps the arrogance and haughty attitude that have existed from some in the Alabama athletic department for decades -and obviously extended to the handling of this investigation and were quite evident yesterday-finally came back to bite the mighty Tide where it hurts the most.

How else can one explain one of the most bizarre endings yesterday to one of the most frustrating and troubling periods in 102 years of Alabama football? If the night of the Sugar Bowl two years ago when Alabama beat Miami for its 12th national championship was the zenith, then what happened a few hours later in Antonio Langham's hotel room and ultimately led to yesterday had to be the Tide's low ebb.

Alabama will go on from here. It will win championships

and enjoy great moments in football. But it will never quite be the same again. For a school as pristine and proud as Alabama, it will be difficult to eradicate the disgrace of the scarlet letter it now carries.

So again, what went wrong?

How does a university that spent nearly $500,000 on legal fees and countless hours of work putting together enough paper to keep a shredder busy for a year be so completely and totally wrong in its assessment of a situation?

How can top officials tell people one day it probably will receive a serious slap on the wrist, then have its legs cut from it the next?

And can a university president such as Roger Sayers -apparently so clueless and asleep at the wheel- continue to allow his athletic director -apparently equally clueless and asleep at the wheel- remain in his position?

Apparently, misery must love company.

It might not be a bad idea when this case is over for the University of Alabama board of trustees to take a long look at Sayers' handling -or perhaps mishandling- of this case.

His angry response yesterday was foolish and simply refusing to admit the obvious. All Sayers was doing was singing to the choir. Perhaps one day, he will come out of the denial stage and admit he blew it.

It is difficult not to empathize with some of Sayers' rage. The NCAA sanctions were outrageous, to some extent, especially in the extraordinarily large number of scholarships taken away.

To some degree, these problems have been brewing since day one. Unfortunately, so many are so used to everything being perfect in a Crimson world, they could not see the trouble that was coming.

And what about the future of Gene Stallings?

Stallings said yesterday he wants to stick around long enough to get back those eight victories (taken away because of the forfeiture). Still, after the dust settles, retirement in Texas might look good to him now.

Yesterday, Sayers said he would not accept Ingram's resignation - even if offered. Again, he was singing to the choir.

Clearly, Ingram's power base has been badly corroded. He stood firm yesterday with Sayers, answering questions about the proceedings.

But he no longer will be free to operate at his own will. No longer will he be held in the same regard.

With the penalties, one must always ask: Will anything be learned from all of this?

Will Alabama be more sedulous in the future when it comes to managing its shop? Or will those who operate what has been the most successful athletic department in the history of the SEC continue to be scornful and supercilious and seemingly above the law?

Today, there just are too many questions and not enough answers. Of course, that is apparently what the NCAA thought all along.

Alabama will move on from here.

The school Alabama always has enjoyed making fun of -especially for its NCAA woes- had a perfect blueprint two years ago after what many thought was a serious blow.

Auburn made the necessary changes and moved on. Auburn officials admitted their mistakes and took their medicine.

They charted a new course with a positive attitude.

Perhaps the biggest challenge of this case is whether Alabama officials can swallow their pride now and look to Auburn for counsel.

After yesterday, looking anywhere for help - other than in the mirror - might be a pretty good start for Alabama top officials after their disastrous handling of this ghastly affair.

JUST WHOSE 'BROTHER' IS HE TODAY?

January 6, 1996

From Brother Bill to Benedict Oliver.

From his alma mater to the archenemy. From the Bear Apparent to working for Buster Brown. This is the saga of Bill "Brother" Oliver, the newest member of the Auburn coaching staff.

Saying that is going to take some getting used to.

Perhaps the most surprising thing about this incredible story is that it really isn't that surprising.

Oliver had been miserable at Alabama working for Gene Stallings. He had flirted with Steve Spurrier of Florida. He had let it be known for months through his spinmeisters that he would not be back at Alabama if Stallings remained.

Maybe it was done in an effort to undermine Stallings and hopefully push the Alabama coach back to his Texas ranch.

But unfortunately, for Oliver, he found out Stallings had more important friends than he did, namely, Paul Bryant, Jr. and Garry Neil Drummond, the president pro tem of the Alabama board of trustees.

That powerful amalgamation easily put down the coup effort from Oliver's infantryman.

Apparently, Oliver then tried to threaten to leave if he didn't get a guarantee from interim Athletic Director Glenn Tuckett to be Alabama's head coach for the 1997 season.

Apparently, he struck out there, too.

Some people believe Oliver had every right to make this move, since the woods were full of whispers that former Athletic Director Hootie Ingram promised him the Alabama head coaching job two years ago. But much has happened since then.

So exit Oliver.

Will he be happier now working for a man he has belittled and poked fun at to all who would listen and nicknamed Buster Brown?

Of course, yesterday, everybody had a good laugh about that.

Like all shotgun marriages, there will be a honeymoon period. But how long will that last? There is little question that Auburn Coach Terry Bowden has hired, arguably, the finest defensive mind in college football. Oliver replaces Wayne Hall, who perhaps ranked in the top three. But a great defensive mind can only do so much unless he has the players.

Oliver's defense in 1992 was regarded as the best in college football in two decades. Most of that team now plays on Sunday in the NFL. This year, many Alabama insiders were predicting the defense would be close to or equal to the vaunted 1992 unit.

However, Oliver's defense gave up 41 points to Tennessee and 31 to Auburn.

Was Oliver too busy grumbling and moaning about Stallings and not spending enough time doing his job?

Whatever, Oliver's credentials are supreme.

But there are a couple of blemishes.

Oliver slowed down Spurrier's high-flying Florida offense on most occasions. Still, Alabama only defeated Spurrier once in five tries at Alabama. Of course, some people blame this more on Alabama's offensive ineptitude than on Oliver.

Perhaps in the end, what has Bowden really proved by taking Oliver away from Alabama?

Does it make him a bigger man?

Bowden already has beaten Alabama two out of three years. He has beaten Florida the same number of times. Same for Georgia.

Does anybody really think Stallings cares that Oliver is gone? Now, one must assume he will give many of Oliver's responsibilities to Mike DuBose, who never really has been given enough credit.

If Stallings brings in former LSU Coach Curley Hallman, one would have to think his defensive coaching staff will be very solid.

Finebaum Said...

Perhaps most important for Stallings, this cancer on his program, propagated by Oliver and his denizens, now will have transferred to Bowden's staff.

Some Alabama fans will be unhappy, perhaps wishing Stallings had retired.

But if Stallings had left, there is some question whether Oliver would have gotten the job. It is interesting that nobody else has seemed interested in him as a head coach.

Openings come and go by the droves. But for whatever reason, other schools have avoided Oliver. It makes you wonder.

However, it didn't make Bowden wonder. The Little Emperor of Auburn has taken away Alabama's best coach. Bowden has gotten the public focus off a crummy 8-4 record and the fact that most of the ties to the Pat Dye era have now been slashed.

But can he trust Oliver?

Here is a man who left Auburn once in a painful departure for the people on the Plain.

Here is a man many people believed undermined the head coach at Alabama. Now, he has left Alabama for Auburn.

Now, he is part of the "Auburn family."

Some family.

All one can do is wish him the best.

But something tells me the marriage between Buster Brown and Brother Bill will not have a happy ending.

SUPERIOR GOLF GAME, BALL COACH

February 12, 1996

Some people have referred to him as the "evil genius." In a recent cover story, *Sports Illustrated* portrayed him as "Coach Superior." But Saturday morning, I simply called him, "Partner." Steve Spurrier, college football's newest $1 million per-year coach, made a quick trip to Birmingham over the weekend on the second leg of a two-day speaking tour to high school coaches for Nike. When he realized the frozen tundra had (mostly) dried out from the ice storm of a week ago, he wanted to play golf.

Roger Bass, a Florida graduate and local businessman, brought along an associate to fill out the fearsome foursome at Shoal Creek.

Since Spurrier had the lowest handicap (3) and I had the highest (no comment!), we became partners in a "friendly" golf match.

I won't bore you with the details of the round. But let me offer this caveat to any future Spurrier golf partners: Don't even think about it, unless your name is Nicklaus, Palmer or Trevino.

Now I know what it is like to be a quarterback for Florida. Perfection is expected. Spurrier has a way of bringing out the best in people. During one four-hole stretch on the front nine, I beared down (though I had not touched a golf club in four months) and strung together three pars and a bogey. I was expecting high-fives from my partner. Instead, he frowned at me. He probably was thinking, "How could he miss those two birdie putts?" During another stretch, which more closely resembled the way his Florida team looked in the second half of the Nebraska game, the closest I came to a birdie was seeing a few in a nearby oak tree and I was lucky to get the time of day from him.

Had I been a quarterback for Florida, I deservingly would have been riding the pine for the rest of the game.

But let me say this: If he has tough expectations for his golf partners and players, the man is much more demanding on himself.

Spurrier groaned more after his own bad shots than a starving bear in early spring.

Attention Florida Gator-Haters: Spurrier never threw his visor down once during the 18-hole match.

When I offered him the use of my Big Bertha after a bad tee shot (he was using a loaner from the pro shop), he snapped, "No, it's not the driver, it's my fault."

Heck, when in doubt, I prefer to blame the driver.

The competitive spirit has been with Spurrier since birth. The 50-year-old coach (who has grandchildren) used to listen to his father, a Tennessee preacher, talk about competition.

"Those who think the object is not to win or lose, but how you play the game, raise your hand," the Rev. J. Graham Spurrier used to ask the congregation.

All the hands shot up. Except his son. "They wouldn't keep score if the object isn't to win," his father would say. "You might as well stay home if you don't come to win."

Spurrier has taken that philosophy through life. It is why many people (including this double-bogey man here) believe he is the best coach in college football today.

"People get mad at me and say I run up the score," Spurrier said. "How come nobody criticizes Rick Pitino when he beats somebody by 40 points?"

Spurrier makes a good point.

Interestingly, Spurrier said one reason some people don't like his style is that he often resembles a basketball coach during a game. He is involved in every play of the game, constantly screaming at his players, coaching them from the sidelines. Much like Pitino.

Five weeks after his most humiliating defeat in the Fiesta

Bowl against Nebraska, Spurrier seems to have shaken it off.

"A loss like that can bring you down to earth in a hurry," Spurrier said.

I believe Spurrier is vastly misunderstood by the news media and the public at large. I don't believe for a minute that he is ego-maniacal. Instead, this is a very confident man who just happens to be an offensive genius.

There is a compassionate and personal side to him, which is very likable.

Spurrier has been fabulously successful, dominating the Southeastern Conference like none since Paul "Bear'" Bryant. But unlike other present-day high-profile coaches, he is quick to admit his faults.

"I used to get all uptight in the past for certain games and the fans did, too," Spurrier said. "This year, we tried to treat every game like another game."

Spurrier kidded me several times during the round about my alma mater, the University of Tennessee. Already, UT fans are treating the battle with Florida in September as Armageddon.

I told him to beware of the orange crowd (it will be more than 100,000) at the enlarged Neyland Stadium when the two meet, which possibly could be a No. 1 vs. No. 2 showdown.

Spurrier looked at me ... and smiled.

"They were pretty excited two years ago," Spurrier said, referring to Florida's 31-0 pasting of the Volunteers.

I quickly changed the subject to the weather.

In all, it was a delightful day. Our team lost the match, thanks largely to Spurrier's partner choking on the 18th hole. But Spurrier wasn't concerned. He had won individual honors on the foursome while I had finished last (he only beat me by 12 strokes).

"Don't give up your day job," Spurrier said to me, flashing that familiar Spurrier smirk.

Steam started to flow out of my ears after that shot. I started to make a crack like, "Hey, Steve, this just in from the Fiesta Bowl,

Nebraska has scored again."

Instead, I shook his hand and did something I'm not accustomed to doing.

I kept my mouth shut.

WILL SHARK BOUNCE BACK? YES, BUT THIS ONE TOUGHEST

April 15, 1996

AUGUSTA, Ga. – Now we know why a network has never before shown a suicide on live television. The one shown yesterday on CBS, committed by Greg Norman, was excruciating to watch both here at Augusta National and certainly across the world.

To watch the man known as the Great White Shark trickle blood slowly and painfully-then, like a leaking faucet- on the velvety lush fairways of Augusta National, was unlike anything anyone has seen.

There have been famous chokes in history. Seldom, if ever, did the gasps involve the No. 1 player in his or her sport. It so unbelievable, so impossible to describe.

More often, it was a newcomer, some Joe Schmo who didn't belong, who had never been in that position. Yesterday, with a six-shot lead at the beginning of the final round of the Masters, Norman looked like someone pulled out of a regular Sunday morning foursome at the club instead of a man who had won 75 tournaments worldwide and has dominated golf. The wizardry he had displayed all week vanished into the Georgia heat as the noose around Norman's neck grew tighter and tighter.

At first, one could hear a faint noise in Norman's direction. Finally it grew louder until the only sound emanating out of

Norman's shaking body was that of choking.

The world's No. 1 player made mistake after mistake as Nick Faldo played brilliantly, leaving Norman staring into the lowering Georgia pines with glassy eyes and a broken heart.

Norman's final round total of 78 (three days after equaling the course record of 63) will go down in golf lore.

Norman summed up his round simply and concisely when it was finally over.

"I played like ...," Norman said, laughing or was it crying?

"I just let it get away," Norman said. "It's very disappointing. I just never had anything going."

Norman admitted the loss hurt, but brushed off questions that it was just something from which he could never recover.

"I'll be back," Norman said. "I'm playing next week."

Asked if he was humanly possible not to dwell on this, Norman retorted: "Just watch. This is not the end of my world. Heck, I just made $38 million (by selling part-ownership in Cobra Golf Company). I'm very philosophical about things. You learn from things, although, I'm not sure I really want to learn from this."

Outside, the rain fell, splashing torrents of moisture into the huge oak tree that guards the veranda of the Augusta National clubhouse.

A sudden-death playoff was about to take place between Scott Hoch and Faldo, but inside the men's locker room, a Great White Shark had just slammed past the swinging doors like a midnight tornado sweeping through a small Arkansas town.

Just moments earlier, Norman had contributed yet another unnerving parable to his legacy, bogeying the 18th hole, missing a sudden-death playoff in the Masters despite shooting a dazzling 67.

Norman stared right at me -I was standing in his path- with a look that said "Get out of my way, mate, or I'm going to bleeping run through you like a windshield through a mosquito on an abandoned highway."

Instantly I scooted out of the way, and after a moment to

check my soaring blood pressure, I cautiously looked back over my shoulder at Norman.

At that instant, he crashed his fist into his wooden locker, and screamed out: "What do I have to do to win this son of a ...?"

It was a question that has been resonating throughout the golf world for nearly two decades.

Tragically-for Norman, at least-they still are asking it today.

The rain and disappointment of 1989 and so many other bloody Sundays at Augusta were on the brink of disappearing yesterday at August, under the scorching Georgia sun amid the most pastoral setting of golf.

What better place to successfully complete the first known exorcism in the annals of golf?

The demons were about to be expunged from the soul and conscious of Norman. Perhaps a man known more for his failures than his amazing grace, was to move on this transcendent Sunday.

Even before Norman decomposed, it was interesting to listen here among the quiet breezes that sweep through the landscape.

Paul Azinger, who beat Norman three years ago in a playoff for the PGA Championship and who the Shark once challenged to a fist fight in the locker room upon learning of a disparaging remark, said:

"Norman has been putting unbelievably," Azinger said. "But how much longer can he do that?"

The answer blowing in the wind at Amen Corner, where the devil jumped out of Rae's Creek and headed straight for the bulging lump in Norman's throat.

One could spend all day discussing which hole (pick any of the 18) where Norman really lost the Masters, but most likely, it was at No. 9 and No. 12.

At No. 9, Norman misjudged his chip shot and to his dismay, had to watch the ball land at the top of the green and roll all the way down the hill.

Then at No. 12, the horrifying par three, Norman made yet

another crucial miscalculation. Disdaining conventional wisdom of 60 years of Masters history, Norman took dead aim at the most perilous pin position in golf.

After his tee shot fell short, and was last seen disappearing into the creek, it was Norman who was dead.

But the crowd continued to cheer, hoping for some kind of miracle shot that so often had been delivered against Norman.

The Shark made it interesting for a hole or two. But there were too many gashes and wounds for his 41-year old body to pull it out.

"I never felt tight at all. No tension in my body or the way I was thinking," Norman said. "I just played horrible."

When his ball splashed in the water at the par-three 16th, one could sense parents across the world turning off the television sets and sending their children away to another room.

There are just some things youngsters shouldn't be allowed to watch. And the public suicide of a Great White Shark is one of those.

Can Norman ever overcome one of the most curious cataclysms in sports history? Certainly, no man in sports has ever had more experience in the unenviable position than Norman.

However, last night as dusk gently fell over Augusta National, no words of encouragement could be enough for Norman.

Perhaps Norman will have some spare time from flying his fighter jets, deep sea fishing or bug-game hinting to read a short passage from T.S. Elliot, who wrote, "April is the cruelest month."

Elliot didn't write those words with golf in mind. But no one are they better suited for than Greg Norman.

MERRY MEX'S SHOTS ARE FOR HIS PARTNERS AS WELL AS GOLF BALLS

May 31, 1996

Gene Stallings was standing on the first tee yesterday at Greystone in front of an imposing mass of people. The subject turned to nerves, which have a way of getting the best of amateur golfers during such events.

I asked the Alabama coach if this was comparable to making a fourth-and-1 call for a possible national championship.

"No, that is nothing like this," Stallings said. "I don't get nervous making the call, because that's what I do for a living."

Stallings paused for a moment, then added: "However, I do get nervous when I have to read about it the next day in your column."

Well, there we were, the odd couple of sports, teaming up for a common purpose yesterday in the HealthSouth Pro-Am.

"This will be the first time I've ever had to pull for you in something," Stallings cracked.

One thing was clear at the end of five hours of golf with Stallings, Jay Barker and incoming Alabama President Andrew Sorensen: none of us should give up his day job.

It was fun, if you enjoy pain and humiliation and incessant chatter from Lee Trevino. Oh, I forgot to mention: The Merry Mex had the misfortune of being paired with this group.

Trevino's chatter did wane toward the end of the round.

"I'm not tired," he said on the tee box of the final hole. "I'm just hoarse from yelling, 'Fore'"

At times, the round was downright comical.

When Sorensen (sans bow tie) sliced his ball into the crowd on the front nine, sending the throng scrambling for cover, Trevino quipped, "How did you miss everyone?"

Trevino turned toward Stallings, saying, "Hey, you need to

sign some of those fans up for defensive backs. Those people were quick on their feet."

Trevino often has been described as a Dr. Jekyll and Mr. Hyde. But yesterday, he was fun to be around.

When you think of Trevino, besides his stellar record as a golfer, you think of his sense of humor. It was evident again yesterday. One of Trevino's funniest cracks ever was uttered just around the corner from Greystone at Shoal Creek, the site of one of his most stirring victories: the 1984 PGA. During the third round, a fan in the gallery was heckling Herman Mitchell, Trevino's corpulent caddie, who wisely missed this round (he has been ill).

"Hey, Lee, what do you feed that guy?" the fellow asked.

Without pausing, Trevino turned and shot back, "Rednecks, and he's hungry."

He came close a few times yesterday to topping that one.

After I hit yet another tee shot in the woods, Trevino said, "Davy Crockett wouldn't go in woods that thick."

He was all over Sorensen, who I hope is a better college president than golfer.

Sad to report, I did not get any news from Sorensen on whom he is considering as the next athletic director at Alabama. He was too busy fishing balls out of the creek.

After nine holes, Sorensen politely shook hands with everyone, saying, "I hate to run, but I'm speaking to a group of Alabama boosters and I need to get to it."

Why didn't I think of that first?

Frankly, I think he was just out of golf balls.

At the tee box on the third hole, Trevino cautioned Barker, a long hitter, to wait to hit his drive.

Sorensen, who is not a long driver, asked Trevino if it was OK for him to hit.

"Hey, Dr. Sorensen," Trevino said, "you could have teed off 30 minutes ago."

TOMMY CHARLES
WAS ONE OF A KIND

August 9, 1996

When the phone rang last night, it startled me. At first, I didn't want to pick it up because I could almost sense by the ring what the news would bring.

"He died," Russ Fine was saying in a soft, barely audible voice. "He went at 7:15 p.m."

As I write this in the wee hours of the morning, I still can't believe it.

I can't believe Tommy Charles is gone.

I can't believe his booming, resonant voice won't be coming out of the radio on WERC like it has for so many years.

What can you say about Tommy Charles in death? I will say the same in passing that I said while he was alive.

He was, quite simply, the best broadcaster this town has ever known. Or ever will.

Tommy had a style that cannot be matched. He had a way to make your blood boil over one minute. The next moment, he could have you crying about a lost dog.

So many memories are flashing through my mind as I sit here thinking about his life. Tommy Charles has two passions - his daughters and his radio job. Watching him sit behind a microphone was like watching a maestro at work. Watching him beam with pride around his daughters was much the same.

I wish I could say that Tommy was a close friend. That we shared dinner together. But I don't think I ever had a meal with Tommy, although I have known him for 15 years.

On the radio, Tommy and I were bitter foes. He took shots at me in the morning. I returned the volley in the afternoon.

Two years ago, Tommy showed up at WERC before my afternoon show and naturally, we began to chat about this or that. We decided to have him open the show and say he had a disagreement with me.

The next thing you know, Tommy was telling tens of thousands of listeners driving home from work that we had a fight in the parking lot, and I was being rushed to the hospital.

I was planning to go on the air a few minutes later and laugh it off as a big joke. But Tommy was so convincing (and so many people wanted to believe he had punched me out), that he stayed on for three hours.

Half of Birmingham believed Tommy had sent me to the hospital. By the end of the show, Tommy had begun to believe it as well.

Although we had a public feud (mostly for show), I respected Tommy's broadcasting skills and he knew it.

Two months ago, at the age of 66, Tommy published his first book. He was so proud of his effort. It was titled "I Hate Paul Finebaum - 303 Reasons Why You Should, Too."

It was a take-off of some books I had previously done on Alabama and Auburn and other college football powers and published by the same house.

Tommy put his heart and soul into the project. I must admit it was a funny book, even if the brickbats were aimed at me.

There were times when I tried to get mad at Tommy Charles. But you couldn't stay mad at this man for long.

There are so many things now I wish I had told him. I wish I had picked his brain for hours upon end about the business and all he knew. I wish I had been his friend. Now, none of that really matters.

All that matters is that he is gone, and I feel a terrible loss.

He was a rare find in broadcasting. He was a genius at stroking people's emotional chords. Tommy was at his best in a crisis.

When an ice storm struck Birmingham in the early 80s,

Tommy held a vigil at the radio station for days.

Three years ago, when the Blizzard of '93 crippled Birmingham, Tommy walked for miles so he could be on the air. He helped people get food and kerosene and whatever they needed.

Less than a fortnight ago, when a bomb ripped through Centennial Olympic Park in Atlanta, Tommy rushed to the radio station in the early morning to make sure someone was manning the ship.

There was nobody better under the blinding glare of pressure than Tommy Charles.

Tommy was also one of the greatest salesmen in radio history. Tommy could do a commercial for a restaurant and make the napkin sound delectable.

We are often told in times of trouble that whatever happens, life goes on. All of us at some point in our lives have seen that axiom hold true.

Others will come and go on the Birmingham airwaves. Eventually, someone else will sit in Tommy's old chair, making an impact on Birmingham radio.

But there will never be another Tommy Charles.

GRIN AND "BEAR" IT, TIDE FANS: SEARCH SHOULD BE NATIONAL

November 27, 1996

Suddenly, he is the man in the spotlight. The man with the unAlabama-like name, but one that is on the lips of every Alabama fan.

Bob Bockrath has been on television this week more than the Thanksgiving turkey. If he makes the wrong decision in hiring the new Alabama coach, some think Bockrath might get plucked worse.

Alabama's athletic director can make this an easy decision. If Bockrath chooses Mike DuBose or someone who has been touched by the paw of the Bear, he can stick around Tuscaloosa as long as he wants. That is, as long as he doesn't interfere with the football program.

Should he dare go "outside the family," according to the conventional wisdom, then Bockrath might as well pack his bags and leave town. If not, perhaps he should head to the nearest Home Depot and stock up on chain-link fences to protect him from all the bricks about to be hurled his way.

In a perfect world, it would be nice if everyone would simply leave Bockrath alone and allow him to pick the best possible coach for Alabama. But you can forget about that.

Picking a football coach at Alabama is just about the most important thing in the world for people who obviously have a lot of free time on their hands.

If Bockrath wants to pick DuBose, good for him.

If he wants to choose Don Shula and allow the retired Miami coach hire every one of his sons to be assistants, then good for him. Obviously, no one in this state appears concerned about nepotism considering half the Bowden family seems to be on the payroll at Auburn while UAB has about the same number of Bartows running wild over there.

The only thing I say about Mike DuBose is the same thing I wondered about Murry Bartow. If these two people were such hot, young coaches, how come nobody else in the nation seemed to have an interest?

There are scores of openings every year and I don't remember either DuBose or Bartow turning down too many jobs. In fact, DuBose got so fed up with Alabama a couple of years ago and desperate to leave that he took a job with the Tampa Bay Bucs. For some inexplicable reason, he was back within a week.

So Bockrath, who was brought to Tuscaloosa after a national search, now is supposed to do the job he is empowered to handle, by looking no further than down the hallway.

That is the easy thing to do. That is apparently what many fans and sports columnists want him to do. But should he do that without at least looking around the nation to see if someone is more qualified?

In a contemporaneous world that is knocking on the door of the 21st century, why can't Bockrath look forward instead of being forced to look over his shoulders toward the past?

Why shouldn't he at least interview some of the best and the brightest football minds in the land before making his monumental decision? Then, if he decides that Mike DuBose is a better choice than Rick Neuheisel or Frank Beamer or Butch Davis or even Gary Barnett, then let us laud the new coach.

But for fans -and especially literate sports journalists- to suggest Bockrath make the announcement tonight and not even search the nation for the best possible choice reeks of fatuous thinking and provincialism at its worst.

Bockrath may have not have grown up in Slapout listening to Alabama football games on the radio while sitting on the back porch, sipping an RC and choking down a Moon Pie. But he has been around football long enough to comprehend what is at stake here in this process. Bockrath hired the easily forgettable Keith Gilbertson at California and the recently fired Todd Bozeman. But one reason Bockrath hired Bozeman as basketball coach was because he was railroaded into it by boosters and a one-dimensional search committee.

Alabama had a basketball opening in 1992 and the usual suspects urged then-Athletic Director Hootie Ingram to hire someone similar to DuBose to replace Wimp Sanderson. In the end, Ingram chose David Hobbs over Bob Huggins of Cincinnati. Right now, Hobbs' team is struggling to crack the Top 40 while Huggins' team is among the best in the nation.

So why don't we all take a deep breath over the holidays and allow Bockrath to do the job he is extremely well-paid for at Alabama without threats and promises of lynch mobs if he chooses the wrong person. If Bockrath blows the selection, his days will be numbered. That comes with the territory.

However, give the man a chance before sticking a sawed-off shotgun between his ears, and saying: "Hire one of Bear's Boys, or else."

TIDE MADE HUGE MISTAKE NOT HIRING BOBBY BOWDEN

November 29, 1996

At 8 p.m. on the night of Jan. 2, 1987, I hung up the phone with the man in Tallahassee, FL. He had sounded upbeat and confident, his dream job finally was within reach, although deep inside, he suspected it already might have slipped away. The lead story on front page of the newspaper that afternoon had centered on Bobby Bowden on the verge of becoming Alabama's coach. I simply was checking with Bowden after he had arrived back home to see how his interview in Birmingham had gone.

But at approximately 11 p.m., something went haywire. Word began leaking out that Bowden was out. I began calling some of my usual sources. Finally, I got a prominent member of the search committee, who had just walked in the door after a marathon meeting with a field of candidates.

I quickly asked him about Bowden.

"I'm afraid we're moving in another direction," he said sheepishly. "Bowden might have a little too much baggage. His age was a factor."

The man hung up the phone without telling me the reason Bobby Bowden had been passed over was because the search committee felt Bill Curry was a better choice.

Today, Curry is out of work and Bobby Bowden's second-ranked Florida State Seminoles are preparing for the most significant season-ending regular season game since 1971 against top-ranked Florida.

Since that foreboding night, Bowden has won a national championship and competed for one every year, including this time around. He hasn't lost a bowl game in more than a decade or finished out of the top four in the final AP Poll. No, that is not a misprint.

I've always wondered how things might have been different if Bowden had come to Alabama. One thing is for sure. Little Bowden probably wouldn't be at Auburn right now.

My guess is that Alabama fans would have warmly embraced Bowden as head coach.

However, it would have been a stretch to say he was part of the so-called "Alabama family."

Yes, Bowden hailed from Birmingham and attended Alabama as a freshman. But he also quit his freshman year at Alabama. He later would spend time with Coach Paul "Bear" Bryant. But still...

One of the major differences between 1987 and now is that Alabama has an athletic director in place who will play a pivotal role in making the decision. If you remember, Ray Perkins served as both athletic director and head football coach and left President Joab Thomas the onerous task of filling both positions. Thomas should have chosen an athletic director first and allowed him to be a part of the search process for the head coach.

Instead, he introduced Steve Sloan at the same press conference at which Curry's hiring was unveiled.

Among Curry's biggest mistakes was only retaining one Alabama person on his staff: Jimmy Fuller. If Bockrath chooses to go outside the family, perhaps one way to ameliorate the situation would be to encourage the new coach to increase that number.

The old joke during the Curry years was that if you wanted to sit around, chew the fat about Bryant and Alabama football, the best place in the state was to go to Auburn.

Pat Dye's staff was loaded with former Bryant coaches and players.

Curry also was a Georgia Tech man with 31-43-4 record. He was 0-7 against Auburn.

I will say this about Curry, though. Along with Sloan, he attempted to bring the family back together again. He rehired John Forney to do the Alabama games on radio. He extended an olive branch to former players and coaches.

To his credit, Curry attempted to clean up the mess left behind from Perkins, who cut the umbilical cord to the Bryant era in one clean swoop of a machete.

It was Perkins who fired the radio announcer, changed the offense, the uniforms, the helmets and the sponsors, such as Golden Flake potato chips.

It was Perkins, an Alabama man, one of Bear's Boys, who ended the Tide's fabled record of 25 consecutive bowl appearances.

Although few people want to remember, the choice of Curry, by many people, was considered a breath of fresh air, a needed change in direction.

A decade later, is Alabama heading in that direction again?

That will be among the issues debated in the coming days as we anxiously await the white puffs of smoke to appear from above Denny Chimes. We'll do that while we're left wondering what might have been if the selection committee hadn't decided a decade ago that Bobby Bowden was too old to be the Alabama coach.

HE SOUNDS GOOD, BUT CAN HE WIN?

December 10, 1996

In an age of cyberspace and cell phones, Mike DuBose came across Monday with friendly familiarity, like a comfortable old shoe or your daddy's favorite rocking chair. What he lacked in sizzle, he more than made up for in substance. As the new Alabama head football coach shuffled to the podium at high noon, one of the calmest transitions in Crimson Tide history took place.

There was no bloodletting. No palace coup.

Instead, it was like Ronald Reagan passing the torch of the presidency to George Bush. Same basic conservative philosophy. But perhaps with more twists and turns and hopefully a few more forward passes.

DuBose does not cut an imposing figure. He looks older than his 43 years and is in dire need of a trip to the hair stylist.

But perhaps his down-home ways are what also makes him such an appealing choice to the people of Alabama.

DuBose didn't bowl anybody over with eclectic words or buoyant promises. In an era of millionaire coaches with super agents, it was nice to see someone genuinely appreciative to have a job.

In fact, no contract has been signed. The details will be worked out later, according to athletic department officials.

In a poignant moment, DuBose talked about his parents and his faith.

In an era of divorce and broken families, it was refreshing to see a man tear up at the mention of his spouse, to speak lovingly of her and with such respect.

Something tells me Polly DuBose won't be dragging Mike out of Alabama practice kicking and screaming to hop in a helicopter to fly up to Birmingham for a James Taylor concert.

DuBose thanked the "little people" who helped make this day possible and that too was refreshing. He made it clear the operative word in Tuscaloosa was going to be "we" and not "I."

DuBose made it clear this job was not a stepping stone. Something tells me DuBose won't have to take time next season before the final game to deny he is going here or there. If DuBose is successful, he will likely be at Alabama until he's old and gray.

While DuBose was the highlight of Monday's news conference, unfortunately, there were a number of low points.

Athletic Director Bob Bockrath's opening commercial for Outback Bowl tickets was embarrassing and out of place.

Perhaps, at Bockrath's former stops of California and Texas Tech, a third-tier bowl game might be reason for celebration. But this is Alabama. For Bockrath to shamelessly hawk tickets for the game took away from the DuBose hiring and the poignancy of the moment.

But the most bewildering appearance -or lack of- was that of President Andrew Sorensen. Alabama's bow-tied president joined the festivities via speaker phone from New York where he was hosting a meeting of the local of the Alabama alumni association.

From this vantage point, his absence was a major slap at DuBose and the football program. Do you think the fine Alabama fans of Nooh Yawk City might have understood if Sorensen had rainchecked for a later date, considering the school was announcing a head coach? This is not an everyday occurrence at the Capstone. Only happened 22 other times.

After all, this is a man who has a private Lear jet at his beck and call. Missing the announcement was bad enough. But apparently, Sorensen's protruding ego wouldn't allow him to completely miss the proceedings.

Sorensen had to babble on about how sorry he was to miss the occasion and how proud he was of DuBose and the invitation to the bowl.

However, for the most part, it was a good day for Alabama, a better day for Mike DuBose. He passed his first major test with flying colors.

Of course, this offering is just one man's opinion.

The most important test for DuBose's tenure at Alabama will be decided in the future on a scoreboard.

BOWL WIN CLOSES STALLINGS' CRIMSON CAREER

January 2, 1997

TAMPA – He moved slowly, as if he had nowhere else to go. He seemed to be squeezing and savoring every last drop of this victory as the now former Alabama head coach shook hands with old friends and signed autographs for little kids. People took pictures. They held up signs.

Alabama fans just didn't want to let go.

He didn't really want to let go.

Finally, Gene Stallings slowly walked up the steps to the chartered bus and breathed easily for the first time all day.

His career at Alabama finally was over.

At 2:23 p.m. CST Wednesday, the buses moved out, heading west amid the cheering throng of Alabama supporters who had gathered for the final farewell.

Someone mentioned, to no one in particular: "It looked like Elvis has just left the building."

An Alabama man turned around and said: "That's right. He means that much to these people."

While these people, these Alabama fans always could find fault with something Stallings did during his seven-year tenure

-whether it was his humdrum offense or his unrelenting berating of the officials, his stubbornness or occasional crankiness- almost every fan loved Stallings as a person. Perhaps that is why so many tears were shed as he made his way through the crowd and into an uncertain world of retirement.

His son, John Mark, put it best as he hugged a reporter who was noting Stallings' every last step. As his father walked by, Johnny whispered: "He's a good man."

Whatever the outcome Wednesday, Stallings would have been fondly remembered by Alabama people. But the Crimson Tide's 17-14 victory against Michigan in the Outback Bowl will help frame the final snapshot, help etch the lasting memory that most people have of Stallings' career as Alabama's head coach.

Stallings got the 70 victories in seven years he talked about so often, although he joked later that 69 would have been fine, too. He won 10 or more games for the fourth time in his Alabama career and averaged the same number for his tenure.

Perhaps most fitting, Stallings' last game was won by the two principles he has preached most often during his career: strong defense and a solid running game.

A big play by the defense and one by the rushing attack spelled doom for the Wolverines and brought joy for all who wear crimson.

The Outback Bowl was not the most exciting bowl game in Alabama history.

But the first half -slow, dull and lacking in any redeeming quality- was suitable for an early rising nation, mostly hung over and bleary eyed from celebrating the new year.

Watching Alabama and Michigan -two programs that mirror each other in almost every category, but most notably in dullness on offense- was enough to send nearly everyone back to bed.

For a while, it looked as if Stallings' farewell would end on a sullen note. I thought for a moment that members of Alabama offensive coaching staff -several of whom are unlikely to be retained by new Coach Mike DuBose- had started their retirement or unemployment a day earlier than expected.

Was offensive coordinator and quarterback coach Woody McCorvey getting revenge? Was line coach Jimmy Fuller sending a message? Was the offensive staff on strike?

But finally, linebacker Dwayne Rudd saved the day, returning an interception 88 yards for a fourth-quarter touchdown that gave the Tide a 10-6 lead.

After the game, in the crowded media room, it was like watching a political fund-raiser to see which muckety-muck could be seen with Stallings most often and be a part of the one picture that makes all the newspaper and television reports.

It was a fierce competition, with many worthy candidates vying for top honor.

But fittingly, Alabama President Andrew Sorensen narrowly won in a photo finish over former Alabama Gov. Jim Folsom for top glad-hander.

Sorensen, whom Stallings never has seemed particularly fond of, looked like the groom's father at the wedding, smiling anytime he came within range of a camera.

Alabama Athletic Director Bob Bockrath, another person who has rubbed Stallings raw, was a no-show for this lovefest. Perhaps with Stallings' entire family gathered around the retiring coach, Bockrath feared for his personal safety.

And so it ends for Stallings. However, before he had reached the airport, the press wags already were speculating on the new staff, on the expected arrival of assistant coaches Neil Callaway and Ellis Johnson, about rumors of who the new offensive coordinator will be.

But even a grizzled veteran couldn't help but get choked up watching the valediction. Stallings came to Tuscaloosa seven years ago with a dubious past and an uncertain future.

During his career, Alabama enjoyed one of its greatest moments, a stunning Sugar Bowl victory against Miami that gave the Tide the 1992 national championship. Unfortunately, the NCAA sanctions of 1995 brought Alabama to its nadir.

But through good times and bad, Stallings had a way of bringing and keeping the family together. That was apparent with the sight of former All-America cornerback Antonio Langham all week in Tampa. Langham, whose signing with an agent early in 1993 put Alabama in trouble with the NCAA, waited outside the Tide's locker room following the game like so many other former players and friends.

Stallings was a throwback. It was a nice change from the new-age nonsense of his predecessor, Bill Curry.

It was interesting Wednesday to note that as Stallings pushed through the cumbersome crowds to the bus, another man walked through virtually unnoticed.

As that man, Mike DuBose, got on the Alabama bus for the final time as an assistant coach, he had to smile. It was his last day in the shadows.

On this New Year's Day, the bright orange spotlight of the sun shined brilliantly on Gene Stallings. It was a fitting farewell to a giant of a coach.

DRIVING 190 MPH NO BIG DEAL

February 17, 1997

Sitting back in my easy chair Sunday afternoon, watching the Demolition Derby better known as the Daytona 500, I couldn't help but smile. I couldn't help but think back to my own evanescent but successful racing career. Back to a time when I took the checkered flag at 186 MPH, waving to the herd of cheering fans who had gathered for my racing debut.

WARNING: This is not a joke. This is Feb. 17. I repeat: This is not April Fool's Day.

For those of you who have followed my career in this space, you probably are saying: Hey, this guy hates racing. No way he's ever stepped foot in a race car, let alone wasted a perfectly gorgeous Sunday afternoon to watch or let alone cover the Great American Race.

Well, the heart of the matter is that I have covered a Daytona 500. And truthfully, it is more exciting to watch on television.

I'm not really sure what there is about the CBS production that it makes the race so enjoyable to watch on TV. Whether it's putting the race-cam in the back of the car. Or simply, the quiet, pensive timbre of Ken Squier and Ned Jarett. Of course, it could be Daytona is the first race of the year and at home, one is safe from flying hoods.

It was also a nice break from the screaming of Dick Vitale. You don't have athletes stomping off the track in protest or angry coaches throwing temper tantrums.

No spitting, either.

You've got the good guys and the bad guys. But the bad guys of this sport look like choir boys compared to the bad boys of the NBA or the NFL or baseball.

Imagine if Jeff Gordon showed up Sunday with orange hair and an earring. And tried to kick a cameraman.

Oh, this sport had some shadowy characters in the past, such as Tim Richmond. And I wonder about some of the fans. Well, make that many of the fans.

But despite all the joking and mocking by people around the nation (blush!), the sport of racing seems to be more in line with the rest of the nation these days than almost any other sport.

Madison Avenue has fallen hard for racing. In this time of boycotts and fan disenchantment, NASCAR has struck a chord with America unlike any other sport.

Sunday's race was melodramatic, despite the yellow-flag finish. But every Daytona 500 is a great race with enough heart-tugging story lines to fill up a soap opera for a month. Oh, I guess by now, you are wondering: Did this writer really ever go around and around on a race track?

Yes, I did. And I lived to tell about it.

For years, Jim Freeman, who until recently was the PR man of Talladega Superspeedway, had talked to me about the possibility of taking a spin around the track. I never really took him seriously. Finally, I got the call one day and drove to Talladega.

Freeman said he wasn't sure I would be able to take the ride. But at worst, we would have lunch at the local greasy spoon (which happens to have the best cheeseburgers in the area) and take a tour of the facilities. So I dressed appropriately: a pair of dress slacks, shirt and a tie. I left my sports jacket in the car.

After lunch, much to my shock and chagrin, Freeman escorted me down to the track and said: "Well, it looks like we're going to do it."

We walked over to Steve Grissom's car and were greeted by Buddy Baker, the legendary NASCAR driver and winner of the 1980 Daytona 500.

I climbed into the passenger seat, sitting on the floorboard with no safety strap (my wife nearly died when I told her that later!). Baker turned the ignition and took me for a couple of spins around the track.

The first time around the high embankment in turn four, I nearly perished from S.S.S. (Superspeedway Shock Syndrome). Remember the most terrorizing rollercoaster ride of your adolescence? Now, multiply it by 10.

I was able to open my eyes for the last lap. Baker looked over and when he saw the first manifestation of color return to a face whiter than that of Casper the Friendly Ghost, he gave me a thumbs up. Then, the driver with a crooked grin slammed his pedal to the metal. I later learned we nearly had touched 190 MPH on the final lap.

So, yes, I have a better cognizance of what the world witnessed Sunday afternoon under the leaden skies and blustery ocean breezes at Daytona. I could only smile as the best NASCAR drivers tried to slingshot and draft and make last-second moves to grab the greatest prize in stock-car racing.

Unlike most sports, which invite you to sit at home and daydream, such as coming to the final hole at Augusta in the Masters or trying to make the winning shot in the NCAA Tournament, I simply shrugged my shoulders as Gordon crossed the finish line to take the checkered flag in the Daytona 500.

For me, it was really no big deal.

For me, it was just another race.

As they say in the trade: Been there. Done that.

NO BETTER MAN THAN SMITH TO BURY THE BARON'S RECORD

March 15, 1997

We come here today not only to praise Dean Smith but to finish burying Adolph Rupp.

Today is the day, the long-awaited day for any avaricious follower of college basketball, when the long, shadowy legend of the late Kentucky basketball coach finally can be capsized.

Let us be the first to throw the last bit of mud on the man and be done with him. It is a travesty to mention Dean Smith and Adolph Rupp in the same breath. To even link the two men through old newsreels and to compare them is laughable.

Obviously, they were and are great coaches who currently are tied as the winningest coaches in college basketball history. But that is about the only common denominator I can see between the two men.

One is honest. A man who follows the letter of the law. Someone fair to all people, white or black.

The other was a charlatan. A man whose program was busted for a point-shaving scandal and received the NCAA's first death penalty when Kentucky was banned from competition during the 1952-53 season. To say nothing of the man being mean and nasty and a racist pig.

And those were his good points.

Arkansas Coach Nolan Richardson put it best the other day when he was asked about the attention concerning today's milestone game for Smith against Colorado in the NCAA Tournament East Regional at Winston-Salem, N.C.

"I never liked Mr. Rupp," said Richardson, who is black. "I never have. Not because he didn't do a great job, because he did. Obviously, he won a lot of games. But I think the world of Dean. He's a class individual. I'll sleep much better knowing Dean is the man."

Rick Pitino, the present Kentucky coach, was asked earlier this week about the great Rupp. One would have expected Pitino to shower Rupp with effusive praise. Not on your life.

"I don't think I would have a lot to offer on that," Pitino said. "There are a lot of people who are better authorities on that than me."

In other words, Pitino was looking for a polite way of evading conversation on that obtuse old man in the brown suit.

Don't misunderstand the point. Rupp was a great coach in his time. Maybe the best of his era. But I was never too sure about his faculties.

This is the same man who helped run off the greatest college football coach in Kentucky history and refused to recruit perhaps the greatest collegiate player.

Rupp was thrilled to see Paul "Bear" Bryant leave Kentucky because he didn't really want the competition for newsprint. Rupp's decision not to offer Wilt Chamberlain a spot on the

Kentucky roster was far more simple: He was black.

Don't look for Nevil Shed to shed any tears today when Smith leaps past Rupp in the record book. Shed played on the Texas Western team that defeated Kentucky 72-65 in the 1966 NCAA Tournament championship game. Kentucky's players were all white. Texas Western's starters were all black in a game often referred to as college basketball's version of Brown v. Board of Education.

It was Rupp's final appearance in the NCAA final. It was forever known as The Night They Drove Old Dixie Down.

Shed had heard the stories making the rounds that Rupp had said five blacks couldn't beat his team. "Well, we just showed him just how tough five niggers could be," Shed would say later. "After the game, he didn't shake any of our hands, not a one of us. He didn't say a kind word about us."

That kind of story almost draws a parallel to another Adolph. Except that one spelled his name with an f at the end.

There are Rupp apologists who maintain he couldn't have recruited black players because of the places Kentucky played in the lily-white Southeastern Conference. And it begs the question: Could Rupp have taken Wilt Chamberlain into Tuscaloosa or Oxford, MS., in the '50s?

Some defenders of Rupp say the racist tag is untrue. They point out he had a black player on one of his teams when he was a high school coach in Illinois. However, Harry Lancaster, who was Rupp's longtime assistant, helps shoot that down in a book on Rupp that was published in 1979.

Discussing a meeting with the University of Kentucky president, Rupp is quoted as saying, "Harry, that SOB is ordering me to get some niggers in here. What am I going to do? He's the boss."

While his record on race was wretched, Rupp left quite a mark in the record book, capturing four national championships in 41 seasons. Smith has only won two titles. But his titles were up against much tougher competition than Rupp.

The Baron of the Bluegrass' last NCAA title came in 1958. Although it was not one of Rupp's best teams (the Wildcats had to defeat Tennessee in the final game of the regular season to qualify), the power of the Baron made his road to the Final Four unconscionably easy.

Kentucky got a first-round bye right into the regional semifinal against Miami (Ohio) and then had to defeat Notre Dame for the regional championship. Both games were played on Kentucky's home court. For the Final Four, the Wildcats had to travel all the way to Louisville, where they won the crown.

If you really want to draw a line between Smith and Rupp, you need to look no further than 1966. The very year the Baron was turning his nose in the air and refusing to shake the hands of Texas Western's starters, Dean Smith was breaking the color barrier at UNC with Charlie Scott.

Smith also helped to integrate Chapel Hill, N.C. at the time by taking a black gentleman into an all-white restaurant for lunch.

Smith was only 35 years old at the time. But he already had passed the Baron as a winner.

TIME FOR FOOLISH FOSSILS TO MOVE ON AT MASTERS

April 11, 1997

AUGUSTA, Ga. – It often is said that Augusta National is a place without a present tense. Any Masters is every Masters.

A walk around the manicured grass is like a journey through an old picture album. Suddenly, a memory flushes through your mind like it was yesterday, with all the colors and smells.

But no matter who you are, whether you are a Golden Bear,

a Great White Shark or a mere Tiger, you can't outrun the past at Augusta National.

It happened to Tiger Woods early Thursday afternoon as he was sitting alone in the men's grill, chomping on a grilled cheese sandwich. Suddenly, an update on ESPN came on the screen, showing the ceremonial start to the Masters earlier in the day with Sam Snead, Gene Sarazen and Byron Nelson.

When the screen showed Snead hitting one right down the middle, Tiger laughed and said to no one in particular, "Not bad."

Certainly, the 84-year-old Snead, winner of 81 tour events and the owner of arguably the most graceful swing in golf history, will be just be thrilled to know Tiger approves of his set up. But such is the story of the Masters, an intersection of generations gone by. If one is fortunate enough to wear the green jacket, you have a lifetime exemption to compete, whether you are standing tall or have one foot in the grave.

One day, although he doesn't know this yet, Tiger will be the old man on the tee.

This agglomeration of past and present is what makes the Masters the most cherished of all sporting events.

And the most ridiculous.

You heard me right.

Oh, some people might say, it is magnificent to see Arnold Palmer, fresh from cancer surgery, strolling up the steep hills of Augusta, thrilling the galleries. Bunk.

Palmer play has become an embarrassment. It was that way before the cancer surgery. It's been that way for a decade.

It was never more humiliating to witness than Thursday afternoon at Augusta.

We all agree Thursday was one of the toughest days to score at the Masters in years, with the whipping wind and greens as hard as concrete blocks.

Still, Palmer shooting 89 (17 over par) is hard to watch. Frankly, it was beyond comprehension.

Of course, Palmer said he would be back next year.

"Want to leave with a better score," Palmer said.

I don't know, Arnie. Perhaps you should get out now while the getting is good. Next time, it might be worse, like 101.

Others marveled Thursday when Doug Ford started in his 45th consecutive Masters. I followed Ford around the back nine Thursday, and frankly, I was embarrassed for his family.

This man hasn't made the cut here since 1971. But there he was, competing along side the Normans and the Faldos for what supposedly is the game's most treasured prize.

Of course, for Ford, it was a very good day. He shot 85 (13 over par). But, at times, it was excruciating to watch, even for a callous critic like me.

On the par-5, 485-yard 13th hole, one of the greatest holes in golf because of its short distance and the risk/reward factor, Ford drove about 175 yards, barely clearing a creek that has never come in play during the Masters. He laid up to 150 yards. I thought he might lay up a third time, but went for the green and barely made it.

It was like watching an aging singer forget his lines during the national anthem before an important ballgame. "I played pretty good," the 75-year-old man said afterward. "I only three-putted six ... greens."

Ford might have forgotten how to play. But at least he hasn't forgotten how to curse like a sailor.

The old line for years about Doug Ford has been that he shows because he can. Finally, someone asked him afterward why he really did. It was a rude question, akin to asking one's elderly grandfather why he drools or passes gas after dinner. But someone had to ask.

"I'll tell you why," Ford said, looking as if he wanted to fight the questioner. "You break your ... leg to try to get invited, so why shouldn't you play?"

Finebaum Said...

Why shouldn't you play? Because any fond memory of a former winner is wiped out after watching such a piteous performance.

This is one time Ford really doesn't have a better idea.

It would be like the Atlanta Braves scratching Greg Maddox in Game Two of the World Series and bringing Phil Neikro in to pitch against the Yankees.

It would be like the bringing Wilt Chamberlain out of retirement and replacing Shaquille O'Neal with him in the lineup.

It would be like putting Bobby Allison in a car and expecting him to chase down Jeff Gordon.

Well ... you get the idea.

Ford played Thursday with Billy Casper, who looked more like a beached whale than a man who has won 51 tour titles on his resume, including a Masters championship and two U.S. Opens. Casper dazzled the galleries with an 83, which included a four-putt triple bogey at No. 2.

Former Masters champions littered the bottom of the leaderboard Thursday.

What is particularly sad is to watch players such as Jack Nicklaus, who supplanted Palmer in the early '60s, begin to fade into the dark and wooly wilderness.

Nicklaus, who has won six titles here, often has said he wouldn't become a ceremonial golfer, competing in any championship if he didn't think he could win.

Earlier this week, Nicklaus acknowledged his chances of winning this tournament probably are over.

Wonder what ever gave him that idea.

Could it have been his opening round of 77?

"I used to listen to Nicklaus say he wouldn't play anymore when he couldn't do it, wouldn't even play the Senior Tour," the crusty Ford said. "Now, look at the son of a ... ."

Yes, look at him. Look at all of them. Growing old can be ugly, especially if you put yourself on public display for the world to see.

A Senior Masters has been suggested as an alternative. Not a bad idea. But something has to give, someone has to get these fossils out of what is supposed to be a golf tournament originally designed to identify the best player in the world.

Granted, the former champions have earned their invitations through the front door. Palmer, Billy Casper and Nicklaus forever have earned a place in our hearts.

However, for the good of the game, someone please kindly show them out the back door and leave it shut.

TIGER PROVING TO AUGUSTA THAT ONLY ONE COLOR MATTERS: GREEN

April 14, 1997

AUGUSTA, Ga. – On this final weekend before the golden anniversary of sport's singular shining moment - the day Jackie Robinson broke the color barrier in baseball - what savory symbolism there would be to see a black man wearing a green coat as the epilogue of the 1997 Masters.

Green and black has never topped anyone's favorite color wheel. Ask any New York fashion designer.

Yet the colors could easily mix here Sunday night in famed Butler Cabin, where until now, the only black faces ever seen are those of the butlers. Tiger Woods is only the fourth black man to ever tee off the Masters. But after two rounds of the most maniacal Masters in memory, Woods is looking like the logical bet to win it all.

Friday here on the cascading fairways of the most exclusive club in America, under thick, silvery skies and a quiet southernly breeze, Woods continued what some once considered an impossible journey.

Woods plays for himself (and Nike, of course). But judging from a handful of blacks following him, he is also playing for them.

As Tiger walked to the first tee yesterday, two black men, wearing badges reading Employee Guest, wailed at him, Go Tiger ... do it Tiger.

Woods quietly acknowledged the men (their faces weren't hard to pick out of the crowd) and quietly said: Thank you. But you could see it in their eyes, in their faces, in their body movement. Tiger Woods was more than a golfer to them - he was the messiah.

In the probable likelihood of a Tiger victory Sunday night, social commentators will ponder the event as one of sport's most important moments.

The winning of a golf tournament by a 21-year old man worth $60 million will be compared to Jackie Robinson's struggle in the 1940s.

A man who is coddled and cuddled by the media and public will be compared to another man, one who was spat on, who couldn't use the same bathrooms, who was called "nigger" when other pejoratives were used up.

If Tiger claims the Masters Sunday, Jesse Jackson will probably be on television faster than you can say CNN.

Jackson probably will invoke the names of Martin Luther King, Jr. and Jackie Robinson.

Who knows? He might even ask Tiger to have a word with the Tennessee governor about getting James Earl Ray a new trial.

Might even ask Congress to name a national holiday after Tiger.

The New York Times will round up the usual suspects, a Harvard professor and perhaps one from Cal-Berkeley, and we will be told it's one of the greatest days for black people since Brown vs. Board of Education.

But in the end, will it really make one bit of difference?

Hard to say, but the paradox won't be missed by anyone. The irony of Tiger Woods winning his first major championship at a golf club once dubbed "The American Singapore" by sportswriter Frank Deford.

Few people who cross through the gates here have forgotten -although many have tried- the contaminated racial past of this club and of this sleepy little Southern burg.

Even fewer have forgotten the charges the club changed the rules in the late sixties to keep Charlie Sifford out of the Masters.

Sifford, who broke the color barrier in golf, has never stopped blasting the tournament, saying it was the worst redneck tournament in the country run by people who openly discriminate against blacks.

The club now has two black members as a result of the notorious Shoal Creek controversy in 1990.

The club said it was already examining the issue at the time of Shoal Creek. Sure, boys, and the check is in the mail, too.

In a one-hour special, Son, Hero and Champion, scheduled to run tomorrow before the Masters, CBS commentator Jim Nantz says of Woods: He accepts a responsibility as a role model to minorities and to the men who came who came before him.

Some have wondered if that means Tiger is a role model to the Charlie Siffords and Lee Elders of the world.

Something tells us he is not. But he is to children across the world, of all colors and nationalities.

Regardless, the sports world waits breathlessly for the conclusion of this year's Masters. Not so much for the golf action but for the social significance.

But if there is a tell-tale sign, a vanguard of things to come here, perhaps it can be found in the flowers, which are almost as famous as the green jacket.

In the past, the dogwoods and azaleas and redbuds -flecked with every tint and tone under the rainbow- have illuminated this cathedral of golf with a shining brilliance. This year, because of an early spring, the flowers are all gone.

Finally, Augusta National is colorless.

Finally, because of Tiger Woods, it is about to become color-blind.

WE ALL HAVE PROMISES TO KEEP

May 31, 1997

Promises, promises. So easy to make, so easy to break.

Such names as Frank Gifford, Marv Albert, Lt. Kelly Flinn, Donald Trump, Dick Morris and Bill Clinton are some of the more famous promise breakers during this recent wave of sleaze. It seems appropriate during this national fascination with the impeached, the organization known as Promise Keepers opened a two-day gathering Friday night at Legion Field.

There have not been this many people in Legion Field standing up and bellowing out the Lord's name since the waning moments of last year's Alabama-Auburn game.

Friday night's featured speaker was Bill McCartney, the founder of Promise Keepers. McCartney is better known to football fans as the former coach of the Colorado Buffaloes, winners of the 1990 national championship. Some people in our state know him best for being on the losing side of the 1991 Blockbuster Bowl against Alabama.

While the Promise Keepers has been widely praised as an organization that has brought families closer together while adding spiritual enrichment, there has been sharp criticism. Of course, that is a common occurrence when the subject is religion.

Perhaps the most stinging attacks have come from special interest groups that maintain the Promise Keepers' primary intent is to keep women barefoot and pregnant, making breakfast and babies.

Finebaum Said...

At some of the early rallies, the National Organization for Women flew banners over the stadiums, reading: Only weak men fear strong women; and Promise Keeper, losers weepers.

Other criticism has been aimed at the organization being lily-white. But the Promise Keepers simply have turned the other cheek.

Instead of wallowing in the mud and fighting turf battles, the organization has grown and progressed with spectacular results, never wavering in its quest to help men become better husbands and ameliorating racial strife.

Considering the current plight of our society, the organization could not have come at a better time. How can one possibly argue with anything that returns America to its moral fiber and reinforces the higher ideals of life?

Ours is a nation founded on the simple concept of making and keeping one's word. Our Judeo-Christian ethic finds its roots in the promises of a God to his people. The standards of that God are grounded in honesty and fidelity and are standards that slowly are being removed from public life.

Furthermore, our capitalistic society has evolved from the honoring of one's word as a basis for business transactions to the necessary priority of protecting yourself from legal exposure.

Finally, the most basic institution in life -the family- now is a refuse of broken vows and unkept promises. The disintegrating American family is producing a generation that does not understand the meaning of words such as honor, integrity and fidelity.

Is it any surprise that our young people are confused about such higher ideals when we consider the aforementioned promise-breakers? These so-called role models of society have set a lower standard.

Consider the claim that Frank Gifford was entrapped into an improper liaison with another woman? Will Kathie Lee buy that excuse? Do you?

Our nation's most famous dealmaker, The Donald, is breaking

one of the most important deals he ever has made: to his current wife, Marla, and their young daughter, Tiffany. Because of an impending choke point in a prenuptial agreement, The Donald has placed a monetary value on his word.

America kept its word in training Flinn to become the first female bomber pilot, only to have Flinn break her word and the military code of conduct.

America is a nation whose strength is founded in the covenant made between its citizens. As citizens, we need to return to the day when a person's word is his or her bond. The truth is told all the time, not just under oath. And our commitment to family, God and country is paramount.

Otherwise, the ultimate consequences of these broken promises are broken lives and a broken nation.

SAY HEY: BRING BACK WILLIE

June 6, 1997

It was a grand time at the old ballpark. The clouds turned an angry gray overhead and rain threatened to ruin the day, but eventually, the sun shone Tuesday. However, for the thousands who made the pilgrimage to Rickwood Field to relive memories of yesteryear, to talk about the way it used to be, the weather was the least of their concerns.

I've always wondered where these people were when former Barons owner Art Clarkson was struggling in his waning years at Rickwood. But we'll save that for another colloquy.

Still, what the Birmingham Barons did a year ago and again Tuesday afternoon is a good thing. It's always fun to be nostalgic.

It is nice to turn the clock back, even for a day. Memories flash back in vivid colors and smells.

However, for all of those people who came back Tuesday to Rickwood, there was one glaring omission. One man who could have turned the place on its heels was nowhere to be found.

Perhaps the greatest player to ever play regularly at Rickwood -perhaps the greatest natural player in baseball history- was sadly absent.

You see, Willie Mays doesn't live here anymore.

You remember Mays. Not many people in Birmingham seem to want to think about him anymore. He was brought up in this community, but never to return again. Oh, Mays has been back.

There was even an effort to redress old wounds a decade or so ago. Sadly, the scab was only pulled apart, with more blood left dripping.

Roger Kahn, the poet laureate of baseball, addressed the prickly issue in his recently published book, *Memories of Summer*.

He spent a couple of days with Mays in California. Naturally, the subject of Birmingham's checkered past came rising up.

Lynching was not a dirty word in Birmingham polite society 50 years ago, Kahn wrote. The dirty word was integration.

Kahn even quotes Mays' father, Kitty-Kat, in the book, conceding that Birmingham is a different city in the '90s.

Things are a lot different in Birmingham these days. They're better.

But not for Willie Mays.

These days, Mays is only spoken about in past tense. There doesn't seem to be a present tense for the greatest ballplayer to come out of these parts.

Perhaps the most telling sign of Alabama's past dealt with a conversation Kahn had with Mays about his football ability. Mays admits he was much better at football than baseball. Scary, huh? Can you imagine Mays as a wide receiver? Or as a quarterback?

Mays played quarterback in Fairfield out of a shotgun formation.

"How far could you throw the football?" Kahn asked.

"In the air? While I was jumping?"

"In the air."

"Sixty yards."

"How many colleges came after you?"

"None."

"You could throw 60 yards in the air? And not a single college offered you a scholarship?"

"I was a quarterback," Mays said, "and I was black."

Enough said.

One would think that Willie Mays has completely shut the door on Alabama. But the author, Kahn, writes a different story in his book.

Kahn describes Mays' trophy case at his spacious California home with 12 Golden Glove awards "I'd have had more," Mays said, "but they didn't start giving them out until my sixth year in the majors", along with other well-known trophies.

Writes Kahn: After a while the trophies begin to blur, until I saw the centerpiece of the display in May's inner sanctum. It was a framed diploma from Fairfield Industrial High School, awarded to Willie Howard Mays Jr. on May 31, 1950.

Willie Mays, now 66, has not forgotten his roots. Even if the greatest ballplayer from this area chooses not to remember much.

Wouldn't it be nice if just one more time Birmingham could bury the hatchet with its dark past? Wouldn't it be nice if we could "say hey" again to Willie Mays?

HIS CAREER ONCE SO PROMISING, GARDNER CAN'T MAKE THE CUT

June 14, 1997

Late at night, as the bugs splatter on his windshield and the white lines of the lonely highways blur his vision, Buddy Gardner's mind often wanders back to the way things used to be.

Back to a more peaceful time before his life became the equivalent of being a roadie in a rock and roll band with too many towns in a row to remember. Bad towns. Horrible towns. Places such as Greenville, SC, and Hershey, PA, and Shreveport, LA.

Never knowing what the next dawn will bring. Never knowing what the next paycheck will be. Or whether there will even be one. Whether this town will be the ticket back to the big-time. Or the last stop on the long and winding road to oblivion. The 41-year-old golfer from Birmingham hasn't hit the end of the road in his golfing career quite yet. But he can see it from his buried lie in a barren fairway.

Gardner started playing the PGA Tour 20 years ago after being an All-America at Auburn. He won the Alabama State Amateur and looked like a sure bet to make it big.

Gardner had some successful years, finishing as high as No. 55 on the money list in 1984. In 1988, Gardner was on the verge of his biggest moment. He led the Houston Open by one stroke over Jay Haas. However, on the 18th hole, Haas drained a miracle 70-foot putt and beat Gardner in a subsequent playoff.

Tough luck.

Of course, tough luck has been Buddy Gardner's middle name.

As recently as 1991, he won $201,700 on the tour. Since then, Gardner's career has become the equivalent of a California mudslide.

Finebaum Said...

Last year, after losing his PGA Tour card, Gardner earned $2,616 on the tour, finishing No. 353 on the money list. This year, he has played the Nike Tour and hasn't done much better, earning $6,461 in six events, ranking him No. 97 on the money list. More money than that passes hands at local country clubs on Saturday afternoon.

On Friday, he shot a 65 in a Nike Tour event in Miami, Ohio, but that followed a 73 on Thursday, so he's 11 strokes behind the leader.

Two weeks ago, it looked as if Gardner was on the way back. He started out like 7,000 other wannabes trying to qualify for the U.S. Open this weekend at Congressional. He breezed through the first stage and appeared set to make the field in the sectional in Atlanta. But he wobbled down the stretch, only to miss making the field by a couple of strokes.

"I was devastated I didn't make the field," said Gardner, who has played in five U.S. Opens. "I really thought if I could get in the Open, I could compete. I really wanted to go."

Seriously, I thought things were going so well, I may win the U.S. Open.

Warning: This is not a misprint.

Gardner really thought he could win the U.S. Open. The man never has won a regular tour event. He can't get arrested on the Nike Tour. Yet, he thought he could win the United States Open Golf Championship, beating out Tiger Woods and Greg Norman and Tom Lehman.

Don't laugh. Golfers are like that. As crazy as it might sound to you or me, this is what keeps them going. It is what keeps someone such as Gardner - given up for dead by most of his friends and followers - out on the tour, competing with a bunch of snot-nosed kids fresh out of college.

Gardner, who has battled injuries much of the past two years, remains optimistic.

"My nerves are good," Gardner said. "The ball is just not

going in the hole."

In golf, that is analogous to the death penalty.

To get back to the big show, Gardner must climb Mount Everest. And he must hurry.

Presently, Gardner is not even fully exempt for every tournament on the Nike Tour, although his veteran tour status usually can get him into a field.

"I want my job back," Gardner said, showing a flare of emotion. "The Nike Tour is tough. I swear it's easier to make money on the regular tour."

Gardner has a point. On the regular tour, you fly to tournaments and are picked up in courtesy cars. You are wined and dined. On the Nike Tour, you are lucky if you can find a Motel 6 where you can sleep and a Taco Bell where you can eat.

"I don't know how much longer I can do this," Gardner said. "I'm sort of thinking this year could be it if something doesn't change."

Gardner, who lives with his wife and two children in Crestline, admits it's beginning to wear on him both physically and emotionally.

And most important, financially.

It costs roughly $100,000 per year just to make ends meet on the regular pro tour, between traveling and hotels. The expenses are a little less on the Nike Tour.

Gardner used to have an equipment contract. Free clubs. Free balls. Free shoes.

"It's all I can do now to get a golf bag," Gardner said. "I'm carrying a little stick bag."

Fortunately, a group of local businessmen continue to support and sponsor Gardner on the golf tour. Initially, they did so with hopes of a big return on their investment. Now, they do it simply out of friendship and respect for their friend.

At 41, the Senior Tour is too far off to even consider. Gardner has thought about becoming a club pro. But he doesn't want to leave Birmingham. He believes he has put enough hardship on his family.

"I'll be 42 in August," Gardner said. "I can't survive for eight years doing what I'm doing."

At this rate, Gardner, who has won $1.5 million in career earnings, will be lucky to survive eight more weeks.

"My ship is sinking," Gardner said. "I've made a lot of money. But in the last five years, I've lost a fortune."

Still, he fights on, hoping to see another day. Hopefully, a brighter day.

"People say golf isn't work," Gardner said. "The hell it isn't."

Hell. An interesting choice of words. One that accurately describes where Buddy Gardner's once-promising golf career has gone.

WATERGATE CHANGED SPORTS, TOO

June 18, 1997

He was gray and wrinkled and looked like death warmed over. I looked closer at the television set. I couldn't believe my eyes. No way, I mumbled to myself. This couldn't be one of my teenage heroes. This couldn't be half of the most famous reporting team in history, the one that inspired my own journalism career in the late 1970s and many thousands of others since.

But there he was the other night on television. There was Carl Bernstein of the famed Washington Post tandem of Woodward and Bernstein, reflecting back on Tuesday's 25th anniversary of the Watergate break-in.

Suddenly, my youth had expired through an hour glass. Suddenly, my once young body began to ache. Where had time gone?

Finebaum Said...

This must have been how older generations felt the day Elvis died. On that hot, August night, I was more interested in climbing over the back fence at Graceland (yes, I cannot tell a lie) with my buddies than in mourning the loss. Besides, I had already turned too cynical to care. As a young pup in journalism, I wrote a scathing column in the Tennessee school paper after one of his last concerts in 1977 in Knoxville.

I had no respect for the icons of society anymore. Not after Woodward and Bernstein brought down the president of the United States.

Besides, Elvis was a fat slob who couldn't sing anymore and had about the same number of pills in his gut as he had glazed doughnuts.

I began to wonder the other night if Watergate had changed it all. Was it a result of Woodward and Bernstein that the world - and particularly my domain of sports- had turned so sour?

Watergate was a sobering wakeup call for American journalism.

Nobody wanted to believe that a couple of police reporters could break the story of the century. Meanwhile, over at the White House press room, the big boys, the ones with the fancy names and Pulitzer Prizes to boot, were left behind with their tongues hanging out in disbelief.

When the world of journalism was rightfully shamed, everyone joined the fray. A faint smell of scandal turned into (suffix)-Gate.

Even in Alabama, we had a couple of Gates, namely, Ramsey and Jelks. Watergate not only changed political reporting but how we cover sports as well.

There are many people who don't like the changes. They prefer to look up to their athletes and coaches as heroes.

Whenever I venture across the line of sports into another venue, I get the same letters: Stick to sports, you bum.

Of course, Watergate has provided the sports world with two

of my favorite quotations. One came from Joe Paterno, the Penn State coach, who years later still was steamed at Nixon for going to the Arkansas-Texas game in 1969 and proclaiming the winner the national champ. Penn State finished the season undefeated as well.

"How could Nixon," Paterno said, "know so much about college football and so little about Watergate?"

Bob Knight said of the national scandal: "When they get to the bottom of Watergate, they will find a basketball coach."

It also gave the expression "deep throat" a new meaning.

Five years ago in this newspaper, I broke the story about the accusations that Wimp Sanderson struck his secretary. It was a big story, one that eventually led to Sanderson's firing as Alabama's basketball coach.

A few days later, I ran into Gene Stallings at a charity golf tournament. I said hello to him, and Stallings snapped at me the way a junkyard dog on the South Side of Chicago would go after an intruder coming over a chain-link fence at midnight.

Stallings said he didn't understand why the story had to be published.

"What's that (hitting your secretary) have to with coaching basketball?" Stallings said.

There were probably a lot more people in agreement with Stallings than with the decision to publish the story.

However, because of Watergate, many things had changed. Like him or not (and I admire him to this day), Richard Nixon was a criminal and had no business serving in the White House.

Wimp Sanderson might have been the best head basketball coach in the history of Alabama. He's a heck of a lot better than the fellow who took his place.

But his actions could not be tolerated by the University of Alabama and couldn't be ignored by a principled newspaper.

Before Watergate, Sanderson's problems probably would have been ignored. Sportswriters -and political reporters, too-

tended to look the other way more than not. There were plenty of cheats and scoundrels back in the old days. But the way they are covered in the media has taken a dramatic turn. Oh, there was great reporting by newspapers over the history of time.

Watergate opened the floodgates. The world hasn't seemed the same ever since.

TAKING THE ROAD LESS TRAVELED

July 19, 1997

"We made a spiritual decision. We had a free ride for 20 years. I felt like I had 20 years left to serve God;" Former CNN sportscaster Bob Kurtz on his decision to leave television and pursue the ministry

It was the time of his life. And what a wonderful life it was.

Deep in his soul, there was the feeling of accomplishment, of being a pioneer in a brave new world. The feeling of being at the zenith of one's career.

He was the first face seen on the inaugural launch of CNN. The kingdom and the glory of cutting-age television were at his finger tips and within his reach.

But deep down, in the pit of his heart and in the bowels of his soul, there was something missing. So he gave it up. Walked away. Never looked back.

This tranquil, diffident man left behind the bright lights and the occasional stage fright. He gave up covering The World Series and the Super Bowl and the Masters. One day, he looked at himself in the mirror and the reflection pointed toward the door.

But what would he do? Would he pursue the dream of his life, to get ready to play the Senior Tour in golf? He was certainly good enough to give it a shot. Or would he look past the dream of his life for the most important thing in his life - his faith? In the end, he took the road less traveled. At 45, Bob Kurtz left CNN to become a minister. Now, some 11 years later, he still has the good looks of an aging sportscaster. But instead of peering in the camera on Sunday night, saying, "Let's go the videotape," Kurtz bows his head from the pulpit Sunday mornings and says quietly: "Let us pray."

He lives in Cullman now, a quiet town off I-65 on the road to nowhere. And he loves it with every fiber of his body.

"I love the parish ministry more than anything," Kurtz said recently. The parishioners of St. John's Church, where he is the senior pastor, feel the same about him.

Kurtz has lived in Alabama since 1993. But his past rarely, if ever, comes up in the course of his life today. Close friends are aware he used to be in the express lane of network television. Occasionally, he makes references to sports on Sunday morning from the pulpit.

However, to most people, Kurtz is simply the minister of the 1,000 member congregation, part of the United Church of Christ.

Danny Woodard, the golf professional at Terri Pines County Club in Cullman, has seen the many lives of Pastor Kurtz. He plays golf with him. He sits in the pew Sunday morning listening to his sermon. He also recently traveled with Kurtz to Augusta for the Masters.

Woodard was able to get a glimpse of Bob Kurtz's life outside the ministry.

"He knew everybody," Woodard said in amazement. "Kurtz knew all the broadcasters and the players. One of his closest friends is Tom Lehman, the reigning British Open champ. Another friend is Steve Jones, the former U.S. Open champion. It was Jones whom Kurtz beat on the final hole of a tournament to claim his greatest golf championship."

And what was the name of that tournament, Rev. Kurtz?

"That," said Kurtz laughing, "was the Bob Kurtz Charity Golf

Classic in Sterling, CO."

Nothing like a little home-cooking, even if Kurtz fired 69 in the final round and drained a 20-footer on 18.

Something tells me Jones has recovered from the beating and was able to get his career back on track.

Kurtz's best round ever is a 65 and has gone as low as 31 on Terri Pine's challenging front nine.

"The pros I talked to at the time told me if had the backing and the ability to practice, he could have made money on the Senior Tour," said Danny Sheridan, the sports analyst for CNN and *USA Today*.

Kurtz had started out his career with the thought of being a minister by studying seminary in college. He did graduate work at Northwestern and began hosting a Christian television program in Chicago.

His work was exemplary, and he began receiving major jobs offers from various television markets to become a sportscaster. One of his stops was Denver, where on a local television station he coined the phrase, the Orange Crush, about the Broncos.

He worked in Dallas before being offered a job as the top sportscaster at CNN. In 1980, no one really knew what to make out of Ted Turner's brainchild, but it sounded like a challenge.

When CNN debuted in 1980, Kurtz and Nick Charles (who is still there) were the first faces that appeared on the screen. The first show on CNN was an interview the two men conducted with then-NFL Commissioner Pete Rozelle.

"Those first years at CNN were the most fun I've ever had," Kurtz said. "Ted (Turner) was downstairs every night and it was a joy."

Kurtz covered all of the big events. He also had a show on Sunday morning (opposite church services) where he picked the NFL games against the spread. Kurtz wasn't just some Joe Schmo picking games. He had amazing grace.

"One year, I was on fire," Kurtz said. "I picked 74 percent against the spread."

Most handicappers are lucky to be over 50 percent.

He was so hot one bookmaker in Chicago would actually change the point spread for the NFL after Kurtz picked because so many people were following his selections.

Sheridan, who publishes the daily line in his column in *USA Today*, also noticed his picks.

"Bob had one of the most incredible handicapping runs on television I've ever seen," Sheridan said. "He was sensational."

Kurtz said he made the picks on a feel.

But one weekend, with national publications and television mediums focusing on his magic, Kurtz hit the wall. He missed four out of five and the jig was up.

So were his feelings for network television.

Kurtz's wife, Pat, was tired of the television life. She thought the people in television were self-absorbed and superficial.

Kurtz loved the life and the people. But the clock on the wall was ticking for him to complete the circle he had started in seminary.

"We made a spiritual decision," Kurtz said. "We had a free ride for 20 years. I felt like I had 20 years left to serve God."

While waiting for a job to materialize in Nashville, Kurtz briefly worked for the PGA tour in the television production end. Frank Chirkinian, the legendary CBS golf producer, urged him to become a television minister.

"There's millions in it," Chirkinian joked. But it was no joke.

At the time, the public was becoming aware just how lucrative the television ministry could be with the bombshells about Jim Bakker and Jimmy Swaggert.

Kurtz went to the Music City instead to preach the gospel. After seven years, the long and winding road led from Nashville to Cullman.

As the Senior Pastor at St. John's, he leads a busy life, from preaching to teaching, from administering the church to administering to the sick and bereaved of his church.

But he has never lost his love for golf. He tries to play once a week and practices whenever he can.

Kurtz continues to pursue his pro golf career, too.

Every year, he packs the clubs for Birmingham and tries to qualify for the Bruno's Memorial Classic.

"And every year, I go to Bent Brook, shoot 74, and fail to make the field," Kurtz said.

He has a long string of disappointments for U.S. Open qualifying, too. Kurtz has not qualified for a senior event in three years although he continues to show up at Monday qualifying for tournaments in this part of the country whenever his schedule permits.

"Golf is a great release for me," Kurtz said, who has two sons-in-laws and a daughter currently serving as PGA club professionals. "I enjoy the friendship and competition."

However, when Kurtz plays his regular game at Terri Pines, his buddies treat him like one of the guys instead of the preacher man.

"The guys we play with curse and holler but he doesn't seem to care," Woodard, the local pro at the club, said. "That's the beauty of Bob."

The church is his life now. The money is considerably less than it was at CNN or could be on the Senior Tour.

"Now, that was a revelation," Kurtz said. "I didn't think people could live on that."

But he has lived just fine, thank you. He wouldn't trade being a pastor in Cullman for anything.

"Even if the PGA Tour granted me an exemption right now, I wouldn't play," Kurtz said. "There's no reason to do. This is my life."

And what a wonderful life it has been.

THIRD AND DUMB

November 24, 1997

AUBURN – Dumb and Dumber. What better way to describe Alabama's offensive coordinator Bruce Arians and head football coach Mike DuBose?

What else can one say about the dumbest call in Alabama football history?

What else can one say about an offensive coordinator who will be fired (soon, please) and a head coach who probably never should have been hired?

It was the perfect way to end a perfectly rotten season. It was only fitting that DuBose, who was unprepared to handle the job of head coach at Alabama in the first place and only got the position through "the good old Bubba network," bungled the biggest game of the year, one his players richly deserved to win.

Instead, the players who laid their guts on the line, had a magnificent victory ripped away because of two dunces masquerading in coaching garb.

If Arians and DuBose were physicians, their decision at the end of the game would have put them in line for a major malpractice suit. The two would be lucky to walk away with their licenses, to say nothing of their reputations.

In any game, numerous plays help determine the outcome. But the "Third-and-Dumb" finished off Alabama.

The most surprising thing was that it really wasn't surprising.

You didn't really expect Alabama to pull this game out now, did you? Why would anybody believe that two men who thought they could win the Auburn game with Freddie Kitchens and Shaun Alexander riding the pine at the beginning would devise a way to hold on to victory at the end.

As bad as it was, in the aftermath of the crushing defeat, one wanted or at least hoped for an explanation, some logical reason for a call that nearly everyone in the stadium knew was stupid.

So what did Coach Dum-Bose say about the most infamous call in the Iron Bowl since Bo ran the wrong way?

"I was not aware of it at that time," DuBose said.

Duh!

"If we execute and don't drop the ball, then it's not a bad call. Obviously, we'd like to have it back, run the ball and punt. But that's not the case. I'm not going to second guess the call at this time."

The operative words there being "at this time."

Of course not. What DuBose will do instead is fire Arians. Blame it all on him. Sure, why not pass the buck when a lynch mob already has formed around Arians? I would rather have heard DuBose be a man and say it was a bad call.

But how would he know? This man is the Ronald Reagan of coaching. Reagan would sleep through cabinet meetings. DuBose sleeps (actually, he just claps) through football games.

Amazingly, some Alabama fans are buying the bull and looking past DuBose to put a bullet in Arians' head.

Talk about looking a gift horse in the mouth. Talk about refusing to cash a lottery ticket. What happened Saturday night at Jordan-Hare Stadium simply is inexcusable and unbelievable. After outplaying Auburn in every facet of the game, after being so close to one of the most stunning victories in school history, why does one suddenly risk it all with a third-down pass?

When you are trying to run out the clock, when you are trying to force the other team to call its last timeout and then have to march the length of the field to have a chance to win -something it had done only once all night- why do you put the ball in the air and force the possibility of an incomplete pass (stopping the clock) or the eventual miscue that stuck a dagger in the heart of every Alabama fan.

Of course, DuBose is living proof of Murhpy's Law. It should be his middle name. As skipper of this Titanic, DuBose can find an iceberg on the way to almost every port.

At least, it didn't really cost Alabama anything important, such as a berth in the SEC championship game or a major bowl bid. Of course, under DuBose, I don't think Alabama ever will have to worry about playing for such stakes.

There will be major staff changes in Tuscaloosa and the rumor mill will be churning with talk for days.

But new assistant coaches can't take away from the incompetent job that DuBose has done this year. For all the whining about the loss of scholarships and injuries, the Alabama players showed Saturday night that emotion has much to do with the outcome of a football game and season.

Unfortunately, at least, for Alabama, it also comes down to coaching.

The Alabama staff made some brilliant calls against Auburn, particularly on the defensive side of the ball.

However, when the game was on the line -when it really mattered- Dumb and Dumber came to the rescue and handed Auburn the victory on a silver platter.

STOP THE INSANITY, PLEASE

March 14, 1998

I can't take it anymore. Someone, please, call this stupid thing off. And do it now.

I can't sleep. I can't eat. I can't work. No one will answer my phone calls. No one will talk to me.

Do I need a shrink (well, don't answer that)?

The problem is the Road to the Final Four. Well, it's not the tournament that is bugging the living you know what out of me.

Finebaum Said...

It's you people out there. Yeah, I'm talking to you. ...

Yep, the folks who put down $5 or $10 in the NCAA office pool. People who couldn't tell the difference between James Naismith and Tubby Smith, who wouldn't know Bobby Knight from Gladys Knight.

Still, you have all converged upon office television sets like the locust plague to such a degree a poor slob like me can't even watch the basketball tournament in peace, at least while I'm at work.

People who wouldn't know Xavier University from Xavier Hollander go loco on Thursday afternoon when Washington beats the Musketeers at the buzzer.

When South Carolina gets shocked by Richmond, janitors and secretaries and group vice presidents all run out of the break room, slamming fists through the wall, screaming expletives.

Please, folks, we're all adults.

I'm stretched out in bed the other night around midnight reading my brand new copy of ESPN Magazine. My wife snuggles up, spring-morning fresh from a steaming hot bath and gives me one of those alluring looks that makes one's heart go pitter patter.

Hmm, I say to myself. Suddenly, the article on Kobe Bryant fades to black. I wait ...

"Would you do something for me?" she says softly.

"Sure, honey," I say, trying to sound like Leonardo DiCaprio.

I say to myself, "Life is good."

She snuggles closer as I shut my eyes in anticipation of her next move.

"Would you help me fill out the Final Four bracket?"

Until that moment, I thought I had the most wonderful, loving marriage in the entire world.

I took a deep breath, as the smoke rushed out of my ears and my blood pressure shot through the ceiling.

"Call Dick Vitale," I said and turned over and went to sleep.

Give me a break!

Finebaum Said...

This epidemic, this scourge that has infected America, has hit home.

You know what is so interesting about this NCAA mania. It could happen to college football, too. Not to the same degree. You probably couldn't have schools like Prairie View or Richmond in a college football playoff.

However, at least it would be interesting and everyone could follow the games for a couple of weeks and have fun. Instead of the dull, laborious, pathetic bowl system we currently suffer through every New Year's season.

The Super Bowl is interesting because it has a two-week buildup (which nobody pays attention except a handful of geeks). Finally, on Super Bowl Sunday, everyone gathers around at some-body's home (hopefully, not yours) and slobbers down food and drink and flicks cigarette and cigar ashes on a new Persian rug.

But the NCAA Tournament is different.

Because of the office pool, everyone has a vested interest. There are debates among the human resources experts in America (another scourge that has infected the workplace) about whether it is good or bad. While most maintain it boosts morale at work, others worry about the "illegal"aspect of the gambling.

Of course, the FBI estimates approximately $2.5 billion is wagered on the tournament.

Illegal money?

Well, trying telling that to the folks who run the "office pool"at the local police station or sheriff's office.

There is even sophisticated software to help make your office pool more user friendly.

All I know is for the first two days of the tournament, from 11 a.m. to midnight, people who normally wouldn't watch a col-lege basketball game unless you put a howitzer to their head are standing around the office television, eyes riveted to the screen, as if the world was coming to an end.

I supposed if you had South Carolina in your Final Four

bracket, perhaps it already has.

So how am I doing?

Sorry, I don't participate in office pools. Against the law. But I do have a vested interest. I'm rooting against every blasted team in my wife's bracket.

The faster her teams get knocked out and life can return to normal around our house, the better my disposition is going to be.

SUMMITT CLIMB WITH VOLS ELEVATES WOMEN'S GAME

March 28, 1998

I first got to know Pat Head Summitt from across the witness stand.

It was nearly two decades ago in Knoxville and she was testifying against me in front of the University of Tennessee Student Publications Board.

You see (gosh, I hate to admit this now, but full disclosure expurgates the soul), I had just been fired as sports editor of the *UT Daily Beacon*, the campus paper. The editor of the *Beacon*, who was a flaming feminist, had mandated me to give equal coverage of women's sports.

At the time, you just didn't do such things in Big Orange Country.

I told the lady editor to take two aspirins and call Gloria Steinem in the morning. Well, perhaps I used stronger words.

She fired me on the spot.

To make a very long story short (although it is a pretty good saga), there was a bigtime hearing, which closely resembled the scene from the movie "Animal House," when they tried to throw the Delta House off campus.

Hundreds of students lined up in a hearing room.

The lead witness against me was Pat Head, who had just arrived on campus as the women's coach.

She argued brilliantly in favor of my dismissal to the applause of practically every female athlete on campus.

Thank goodness, men still had a say in society back then and the board voted 8-0 in my favor and gave me the job back (and subsequently fired the lady editor).

How times have changed!

Today, if someone tried to go up against Summitt at UT, he or she probably would be run out of town.

Summitt is the women's version of John Wooden, only she probably is a better coach. Others have compared her no-nonsense, tough discipline to Bear Bryant.

She once made her team practice the day after a loss in the same stinking, sweat-soaked uniforms they had played in the night before.

"You didn't play the second half last night, so you owe me 20 minutes today," she said.

I can see Bryant smiling about that story.

What Summitt has accomplished defies logic. Incredibly, she has turned a fairly boring sport - sorry, but there is no comparison to men's basketball - into a happening.

Signs at UT games this year read: "We're not fans. We're a cult."

The team, and its coach, were the subject this week of an HBO documentary. Two weeks ago, Summitt was featured on the cover of *Sports Illustrated* - the first time ever for a women's coach.

On Thursday, *The New York Times* had a story on the front page about Summitt and her team's quest. Yes, right under the Jonesboro shooting and the latest dirt on Clinton's intern(al) problems.

In addition, Broadway Books has just published Summitt's

autobiography, "Reach For the Summit." It's a fabulous book describing her life story and her strategy for success.

At the rate she is going, they'll soon be saying "Peyton Who?" in Knoxville, if they're not doing so already.

My favorite Summitt story concerns her pregnancy seven years ago. Against everyone's advice, particularly her physician, Summitt jumped on the school plane to visit a recruit, Michelle Marciniak in Pennsylvania. During the visit, her water broke. When she got to the house, the family asked: "How are you doing, Pat?

"I'm in labor."

Upon hearing that, the family was in need of seeing a doctor.

Summitt began having full contractions at the recruit's home. Finally, she wrapped up the visit, took off on the plane and realizing the baby was close, the pilot radioed ahead to the nearest airport in Roanoke, Va., and requested an emergency landing.

Upon hearing this, Summitt went crazy, or crazier than she already was (because of the labor).

You see, Tennessee had lost to Virginia in overtime a few months earlier in an NCAA Tournament regional final. It cost the Vols a trip to the Final Four, which was held in Knoxville.

Summitt refused to have her son in Virginia. They made it back to Knoxville in the nick of time.

At 45, Summitt has reached the pinnacle of her career. Shooting for her school's sixth NCAA title this weekend in the past 12 years, she has compiled a winning percentage of .815. This season, the Lady Vols averaged 14,952 fans per game.

Did the Alabama men draw that many fans all season?

Summitt doesn't use tired old rhetoric to fight for women's rights or social issues. She does it with action.

As I have admired her over the years, mostly from a safe distance, I often think back to that sunny spring day in Knoxville in the late 70s, the day we went to war over an issue.

In some ways, I am proud to have scored a victory over the

lady who never seems to lose. At times, I am embarrassed.

Perhaps one could reach deep down into the book of cliches and say that I won the battle against Pat Head Summitt on that particular day.

ONLY TIME CAN HEAL WOUNDS LIKE THESE

April 11, 1998

The following space on this particular place on the calendar usually has been reserved for the Masters. But as this is being written on Good Friday, the thought of Augusta seems distant, like a faraway berg in a long forgotten place.

Rushing on Friday morning to pick up a slew of newspapers that arrive at our residence every day, instinctively, I turned for the sports page. However, there it was, on the front page of the *New York Times*, a story next to a picture of the massive tornado wreckage in Alabama with a man - wearing a 1957 Auburn national championship sweatshirt - who had found an American flag in the rubble.

There was the all too familiar dateline of Birmingham, Ala. Only this time, it had nothing to do with a church bombing or the explosion at an abortion clinic.

This cataclysm, this massive loss of life and property, was a crime of nature. Yet, the end result was similar to those who perpetrated the bombings of our past, leaving death, destruction and heartbreak in our memory forever.

After a bombing, one can think back and try to understand the motivation. We can send our best reporters and talk to the families of the accused, hopefully to get a better grip on why someone would commit such a cowardly act.

With something like this, one can only depend on the weather people to analyze the storm, to put a numerical classification on the twister. Of course, to the people who lost their lives, what difference does it make now whether it was F-4 or an F-5?

Still, we must praise those in the news media, those who helped get the message out, who calmly but firmly urged a community to seek shelter from the storm.

We must agree continuous weather coverage Wednesday night saved lives. It is easy to criticize our friends who stand in front of the blinking weather maps with their million-dollar radar screens, screaming "the sky is falling" when a snowflake is spotted on the Mississippi-Alabama border.

This time, they screamed early and often and fortunately, many people heeded their warnings. The sky wasn't falling this time. Tragically, it was our homes and churches.

Lifetimes of hard work were reduced to what could fit in the back of a Chevy truck. No answers. But for every story of heartbreak, there was one of hope.

For the lost lives, there were stories such as Rev. Rick Cooper of the Open Door Church, where the roof of his chapel was blown off but everyone attending Wednesday night services survived.

"We had faith," he said. "It was a miracle."

In trying to sort through the shattered buildings and broken dreams of these past few days, one couldn't help but think back to the tragedy that struck another Alabama town four years ago on Palm Sunday. Who could ever forget the tornado that wiped out Goshen United Methodist Church in Piedmont, killing 20, including the daughter of Rev. Kelly Clem?

She said something at the time and it still resonates today:

"This might shake people's faith for a long time. I think that is normal. But having your faith shaken is not the same as losing it."

Clem said God did not send the storm that killed her precious child. Her husband, also a minister, added: "My God is a God of hope. It is never his will for anyone to die."

I think about those comments often when I see destruction and death. I have thought of the same things in my own life, losing a father at 15 and a dear mother three years ago.

But I'm one of the lucky ones. And so are most of you.

Most of us have never walked into our den to turn on the television, only to hear the sound of a freight train rumbling overhead and in a nanosecond, have the roof and all our belongings blown apart and shattered forever.

We look at the television and grimace. We look at the ghastly pictures and frown. We say we feel their pain and promise to pray for the less fortunate.

But do we know how they feel?

Standing at my father's newly dug grave on a cold, blustery March day at the tender age of 15, I remember a friend walking up, saying: "I'm so sorry. ... I know how you must feel."

Sure, I mumbled to myself. He doesn't have a clue. My life is over. My father's gone. We won't have any money and I won't be able to go off to a good school and make something of my life.

However, my life wasn't over. It was just beginning. The pain was searing. But a long and dark and often lonely road in the wilderness eventually led to happiness and a good life.

Words alone are not enough to comfort those who have suffered in our community. Only time can heal the pain and heartache. Let us all hope and pray on this holy weekend that time is short.

NASCAR A LOSER ON RACE

April 25, 1998

On my first visit to the Talledega track to cover the big race, I remember picking the brain of a fellow sportswriter. The man seemed to have a passion for the sport, so I asked him what made it so special to him.

The sportswriter looked at me and, with a sly grin, said: "Two reasons. They bring the winner up to the press box after the race. And there ain't no (blacks)."

Through the years, we have all watched NASCAR grow into one of the most successful sports on the map. Now, according to recent reports, it has become a $2 billion-per-year business, with races as far away as Japan. It's come a long way from a bunch of moonshine boys on a dirt track.

NASCAR officials never miss a chance to boast about the meteoric growth of the sport. Interestingly, they don't talk very much about the predominant color of the drivers or of the millions of fans who watch the sport every year.

Which begs the question: Is NASCAR the last bastion of racism on the American sports scene? And perhaps a bigger and more important question: Do the people who run the sport really care and perhaps even cater to the lily-white image?

"I've been in this business for 40 years," said Dr. Jesse Lewis, the owner and publisher of *The Birmingham Times*, the community's largest and most influential black newspaper.

"In that time, I have never received a press release, a press pass, an invitation to sit in the press box, an invitation to play in their golf tournament. Nothing from these people. They don't want black people around. I know ... well they send everybody else one. They are the worst in the world."

Lewis said he wrote Bill France Sr., the founder of NASCAR, about 15 years ago with his complaints.

What did France say?

"He never wrote me back," Lewis said.

Several months ago, Bill France, Jr., the president of NASCAR and son of the founder, was asked by *The Charlotte Observer* about a lack of racial diversity in his sport.

"We don't view that as an issue," France said. "Anybody can be anything regardless of your race or your origin. You can't wave a magic wand and make everything happen that somebody wants to happen."

In the 50 years of NASCAR racing, only six black drivers have made it to the Winston Cup circuit. Only one of them, Wendell Scott, won a race. Even then, the officials initially gave another driver the trophy because it was feared the crowd would mutiny if a black man was honored afterward. Later, when the grandstands were empty, Scott got the trophy.

His career ended in 1973 after he was injured at Talladega.

Grant Lynch, the man who operates Talladega Superspeedway, said there are no racial biases. He seemed surprised this week someone would even raise the question.

"Hey, there is no active barrier," Lynch said. "The sport is open. Julius Erving and Joe Washington operate a Busch team and NASCAR is behind that."

Talladega officials also boast about the fact that people from practically every state come through the speedway entrance. But racing officials go mute when it comes to telling you what color the people are going through the gate.

"There is no way of checking ethnic origin," Lynch said.

Lynch said the track simply markets its product to race fans, without concern of race.

"We basically go where we sell a lot of tickets," Lynch said. "We run generic ads not based on ethnic (makeup)."

Asked if Talladega had ever bought advertising in his paper, Lewis responded:

"Hell, no," Lewis said. "The truth of the matter is, they are not interested in appealing to blacks. They get one caliber of people to their races. They don't give a ... about anybody else. They don't attract top-of-the-line people. They don't want black people there of any kind. If they wanted black people, they would invite blacks to their event."

For the most part, NASCAR is a family affair. At least a dozen brothers currently are competing today and family legacies, such as the Pettys and Allisons, are more prominent in this sport than any other.

Of course, the biggest reason NASCAR has not reached out for blacks is simple: The organization doesn't have to.

"There probably hasn't been as much looking into (attracting blacks), in all honesty, because the seats have been full," France said last year. "If 25 percent of our seats were empty, a good entrepreneurial, free-enterprise America would look around and say, 'Who can I get to fill those seats?'"

John Griffin, the director of communications for NASCAR, scoffed this week at the suggestion that Frances' comments were tinged with racism.

"Rightfully, or wrongfully, that's how it's been done in past," Griffin said. "As we continue to grow, you'll see us going in that direction."

Exactly what direction Griffin is talking about is unclear, although one can only hope it's different than the one NASCAR has gone in its first 50 years.

Griffin points out it is difficult to interest young blacks in NASCAR compared to other sports.

"It's easy for baseball, tennis or golf to leave some stuff in the inner city like tennis racquets or balls or bats," Griffin said. "It's hard to leave a race car."

As we close in on the next millennium, the question being raised is simple: Is NASCAR the last bastion of racism on the American sports scene?

"I don't think saying that would be a fair statement," Griffin said. "Certainly, there are minorities at our events."

However, while Griffin was quick to point out a recent survey showed 38 percent of NASCAR fans are women, he was unable to provide a number for blacks.

"Our sport seems to be very attractive to white middle America," Griffin said.

And until further notice, that seems to be just the way folks at the Talladega Superspeedway and at NASCAR headquarters in Daytona want to keep it.

CHANGES WOULD MAKE BEAR ROLL IN HIS GRAVE

July 11, 1998

I fought sleep with vigor. It was a losing battle.

Larry Langford was on the tube speaking of his mother on the MAPS infomercial.

"My mama didn't have an education, but she had a lot of common sense," Langford was saying now. "She told me if you always do what you've always done ..."

The lights went off and my mind began to wander. As best I can remember, I fell asleep and had the following dream.

Suddenly, I was at the gravesite of Paul "Bear" Bryant in Elmwood Cemetery. Thunderstorms rumbled in the background while bolts of lightening dashed through the black sky like a Fourth of July fireworks demonstration.

I felt the ground shake for a moment. Finally, I heard a voice.

"So you are back."

It was the deep, gravelly voice of the Bear.

"Yes sir, Coach," I said.

"Where have you been?"

I was speechless. After his death in 1983, whenever friends came to town, I would take them to the cemetery. However, like everything else, his memory began to fade and I took friends to all of Birmingham's newer attractions like the Turf Club, the USFL, the World League and the CFL games, as well as to see our CBA team.

"Do you still follow Alabama football?" I asked.

"Nope", said the Bear.

"Quit watching when Curry was hired. What a fraud. When he said I wanted him to replace me when I retired, I gave up and became a half-hearted Auburn fan."

"An Auburn fan?" I asked.

"Well, most of my former coaches were down there until Pat Dye resigned. However, reality struck me and I quit being an Auburn fan when they hired that little snot-nosed Bowden. I remember him when he was two feet tall."

"He still is, Coach Bryant," I said.

"Well, I'm a Spurrier man now. Even bought one of those Gator snoots."

I tried to imagine the Bear wearing one of those but quickly changed the conversation. I told Bryant about the national championship in 1992 and he seemed very pleased to hear that.

"You heard about Wimp Sanderson?," I asked.

"Nah, did that old rascal ever get past the Sweet 16?"

I explained Sanderson had been fired over the incident with his secretary.

"They fired him for that?"

Bryant became very disturbed when I told him about the NCAA sanctions concerning Antonio Langham.

"The nerve of them. I wish someone would have let me know. I would have called Walter Byers and taken care of that in five minutes."

I told Bryant that Byers was no longer in charge of the NCAA and he finally calmed down.

"So how's Bebes doing down there now?

I explained the new president, Dr. Andrew Sorensen, and Athletic Director Bob Bockrath had run him out of town after averaging 10 victories a year for seven seasons.

"Now, Bockrath, isn't he that guy that spoke to the Mobile Touchdown Club a couple of months after he got the job and made a statement implying that I didn't go to school at Alabama. How could they have hired a knucklehead at Alabama to run the program that didn't even know I went to school there. Where did he come from?"

"He came from California and Texas Tech where both schools got in serious trouble with the NCAA. Alabama is currently under investigation in basketball."

Bryant didn't seem overly concerned so I changed the subject.

I told him about Brother Oliver going to Auburn as defensive coordinator.

"Next thing you'll tell me Alabama is playing the Iron Bowl down there at Jordan-Hare."

When I told him that was true, he was outraged.

"Unbelievable. I once swore if we ever played down there it would be over my dead body."

I began telling Bryant about the most recent game on the Plains. When it was mentioned how Alabama lost the game on a screen play and Mike DuBose admitted he didn't even know the call, Bryant interrupted me.

"Why the .... was DuBose even talking about it? He's a defensive line coach."

I broke the news DuBose was now head coach.

"Mike DuBose is the head football coach at the University of Alabama. You've got to be kidding. He couldn't win four games as a head coach."

"Well, as a matter of fact Coach Bryant, he went 4-7 last year in his rookie season," I told him.

I began describing the seven losses in vivid details, including the ones to Arkansas, Kentucky and Louisiana Tech. But after a great recruiting year, I told Bryant things were looking up for 1998.

"Are we ranked preseason No. 1 then in the AP poll?"

"No coach."

"Well, that's okay. I always liked it when we they tried to teach us a lesson in the preseason and had us way down to No. 2 or No. 3. That always fired up the boys."

I didn't have the nerve to tell him Alabama wasn't even in the top 25. Bryant asked me what I was predicting for the upcoming season. I told him Alabama fans were all over me because I had picked the Tide to go 7-4 back in spring.

"You .... right they ought to be all over you. Picking us that low."

"Excuse me, Coach. But Alabama fans are upset because they think I have raised the bar too high. They don't even think Alabama will have a winning record under DuBose."

"Oh, really. That is beyond my comprehension."

I could tell the conversation was over and thanked Coach Bryant for his time.

"Oh, one more thing," Bryant said. "How's Simpson Pepper doing with the PA? Boy, he's good."

"Coach, Bockrath fired him."

"I don't believe it. This Bockrath fellow is lucky I'm not still now around. Well, at least he hasn't changed our beautiful crimson uniforms they make down at Russell."

"Uh ... yes, Coach, the Nike swoosh is now on everything."

Bryant was silent for a moment.

"Well, at least Coke is still involved in the program."

"No, Coach, Pepsi is now the soft drink of the Tide."

"Boy, things have really changed. But you still can't beat the Tide at Bryant-Denny."

I thought for a moment.

"Uh, Coach, Alabama had problems at home last year.

"What, we lost a game? I don't believe it. I only lost two games there in 25 years."

"Uh, Coach, Alabama lost all four home games in 1997."

I began walking away at this point, realizing Bryant was upset.

"Hey, hold on a second," Bryant said. "This Bockrath fellow hasn't taken my name off the stadium and sold it to a hamburger chain, now, has he?"

Not yet. But I warned him the summer was still young.

A YEAR AFTER HIS DEATH, FORNEY'S LEGACY STILL LIVES

July 25, 1998

On the dining room table in her modest Homewood condominium, the stack of mail gathers dust.

"I haven't eaten off it in a year," Marjorie Harrison Forney is saying now, slowly and painstakingly and tinged with sadness. "It's the sympathy card table. There were 2,000 letters to start with. I'm almost done writing everyone back."

One year after his sudden death, John Forney's widow is still trying to cope with the loss of her husband.

"Life without John has been very dismal,"she said, her voice drowning with emotion. "It is just so sad without him."

So sad, indeed.

For his friends and colleagues -even for those who only heard him but never met the legendary Alabama broadcaster- the past year has been miserable.

Not to see his friendly face. Not hearing the soothing voice, that slow, Southern drawl that blended in with the crowd noise from Legion Field on those crystal blue October Saturdays.

You could sit in your living room or on the front porch steps in the backwoods and listen to him call the action and think you were there. He often gave the wrong information. Often, he was difficult to understand. But it didn't really matter.

He was Alabama football.

It has been a tough year for Forney's thousands of friends and admirers. But leave it to Forney to have a good year - even after he's gone. I can almost hear him in heaven, having a drink with Coach Bryant, laughing about that one.

He finally was elected into the Alabama Sports Hall of Fame. His books on Alabama football continued to sell.

Countless organizations, too many to mention, have given scholarships in his name and honor. Most important, at least, for his family, Forney's legacy lives on.

"I have just been overwhelmed by the reaction," Mrs. Forney said. "The community has remembered him so fondly. I get letters every day. And wherever I go, people come up to me."

While the attention has been touching, it also can make the grief more unbearable.

"Some of the stories are just so heart-wrenching that it makes me sad," she said. "It brings up so many memories. It is sort of a paradox: so wonderful, but also so emotional."

Mrs. Forney said she has been especially touched by the people who didn't know her husband, which reminded one of an article done the day after he died.

Bob Johnson wrote in the *Birmingham Post Herald* of Forney's death and told the story of this man from a disparate perspective.

Johnson knew a different Forney than those of us who carried the casket through the gates of Elmwood Cemetery on that sweltering summer day. He never met Forney. But, oh, did Johnson know him.

Johnson wrote of growing up listening to Forney in South Alabama, of being an Army brat and hearing the voice over Armed Forces Network as far away as Hawaii and Turkey. He wrote of growing older, of finding out Santa Claus was just a man in a red suit and discovered Alabama football was a business when school officials fired Forney as the Crimson Tide's football announcer.

"But you know, even though it's not quite the same, I still love Christmas and Alabama football," Johnson wrote. "And John Forney still loved Alabama football right up to the day he died. ... And just like I sometimes still hear Santa's sleigh bells on Christmas Eve night, I'll always believe that if I turn the radio dial long enough, I'll find John Forney's voice somewhere in the static."

Now, late at night, the voice often is heard in the living room where the din of his laughter and the comfort of his love once reigned.

Often, Mrs. Forney sits in a darkened room, staring at the television. As she flips through myriad stations, the still of the night is broken with a vision and sound on the screen, a haunting reminder of the love of her life.

It is John Forney -smiling at her- reliving the glory days of Alabama football. The television program she occasionally finds with the remote control is titled "Bama's Greatest Games," with Forney serving as the host. It still runs frequently on cable television.

"I look up and there he is, looking just like the day he left Earth," Mrs. Forney said. "I forget when I see him that he won't be coming home."

Marjorie Forney is tiring now. She is tired because of the late hour and she is emotionally spent from having to relive the tragedy.

Losing her husband has been so difficult, especially coupled with her own mother being seriously ill in Kentucky.

She has been to grief support. She has spoken to friends, been comforted by family.

But the agony of losing someone as special as John Forney won't go away.

"There's still such a void and such sadness," she said. "He was just the same in public as he was in private - so caring and compassionate.

"It is just so hard to live without him."

LIKE BRYANT, HE DEFINED A PAST THAT WE CAN'T ESCAPE

September 18, 1998

As a young boy growing up in Memphis, the two raging images I had of Alabama were of George Corley Wallace and Paul "Bear" Bryant.

One man was hated. The other feared.

Now, both men are gone.

Yet, in many respects, their colorful and controversial images live on, seared in the American tableau.

Alabama has a Mercedes plant. We have a Civil Rights Museum. Yet, our heads are still pointed backwards, in many respects, because of these two men.

The politics of race still haunt the state. On the sports scene, the stubborn refusal, the inability, to let go of Bryant still torments us.

Despite all the rhetoric this week of repentance and remorse, many of the same people who elected George Wallace four times are still calling the shots at the ballot boxes.

On the sports front, Mike DuBose came to a local football group this week, opening his speech by quoting Bear Bryant.

Don't misunderstand the point.

Finebaum Said...

Both Wallace and Bryant were great men in their day. Many lessons, both good and evil, can be learned from the two most important and influential figures in our modern state history.

There were many differences between the two men - particularly on race.

Wayne Flynt, the distinguished Auburn professor, once said that "no one has done more to promote racial harmony in Alabama than Bryant."

After Sam Cunningham, a black running back at USC, ripped Alabama's defense apart in a memorable 1970 game at Legion Field, it was Bryant who observed: "Cunningham did more for integration in 60 minutes than Martin Luther King did in 20 years."

Still, one has to wonder when this state will move on. When will we be brave enough to chart a new course, see the dawning of a new day, without evoking the memories of Wallace and Bryant?

Many of the same people in Birmingham who blame George Wallace for blocking the completion of the interstate system for our town praise Bryant for keeping the NFL out of here.

Good for Bear.

Instead of having the Tennessee Oilers in town this weekend at Legion Field, we have Tennessee Tech.

Bryant had every right to be selfish. Why did he want a pro team in Birmingham competing with his kingdom and glory?

When Gene Stallings retired two years ago, the search for his replacement resembled a Grade B movie.

DuBose was an Alabama man. He played for Bryant. Therefore, there was no reason to look outside the family.

Why hire the best man when you can hire a Bryant man?

Has it worked out? Who knows?

Alabama seems to be moving forward two games into a second season following a 4-7 record. But there are nine more games to go filled with trials and tribulations.

Finebaum Said...

One couldn't help this week to draw comparisons to the passing of Wallace and Bryant and their respective funerals.

Two cocky and arrogant rivals for the affection of Alabamians in their prime, Bryant would have perhaps, been proud to know he drew far more adulation and commotion at his passing than Wallace.

Of course, Bryant's funeral took place less than a month following his final game. His image still burned bright. Wallace's death occurred a dozen years after he left office and more than a quarter century after the zenith of his storied political career.

Bryant fought off retirement because he knew what would happen.

"Quit coaching?" Bryant once said, after being asked about retirement. "I'd croak in a week."

I have always felt Bryant was fortunate to go so quickly. Even in retirement, he would have been a presence. But I don't think he would have enjoyed seeing someone else at the center of attention.

Perhaps, had Bryant lived longer, it would have been easier for the school to escape his shadow. At some point, perhaps, he would have encouraged Alabama to bring in a new man from the outside, to change the direction of the school's football program. But I doubt it.

In Wallace's case, he could really never let go, either. He should not have run again in 1982 for governor. He was sick and weak, a feeble man who could no longer do the job. But he was bored so he asked for and received "a last hurrah."

In certain respects, we are still paying for the gesture.

In Bryant's case, there has been a price as well.

For all he gave us, his legacy continues to weigh Alabama football down like a ball and chain. Every Alabama coach, whether he wants to or not, has to bow down to Bear Bryant in the morning, afternoon and evening to maintain his popularity and respect.

As we approach the next millennium, perhaps, this state can move forward both in politics and in sports to produce a new beginning, a century of looking forward instead of hanging on to a fading and distant past.

SLINK HOME, ALABAMA

September 28, 1998

We come here today not to bury Mike DuBose but to praise him. To praise him as a man of his word. A man of high integrity. A man of honor and principle.

The second-year head coach vigorously promised to return Alabama to the way it used to be. He made the necessary coaching changes. He made the adjustments.

He has delivered.

Alabama has returned to the past: 1957.

DuBose decided to skip the Bryant era in this trip down memory lane. Forget Stallings, Perkins and even Curry while he has us sailing through the time tunnel.

Let's take Alabama back to the era of "Ears" Whitworth. And do not pass go. Why worry about the future when we can relive the past?

DuBose has done it all. He has ripped off the starched shirt and tie and replaced it with sweaty, stinky golf shirt. He has quit coaching by committee and started sticking his nose in everybody's business. He has put on the headsets and become more involved in the play-calling.

You have to be kidding.

It is too late to get Bruce Arians back on campus. It is to late to beg his forgiveness for all the rotten things said about him. The last time we saw him, Alabama was moving the football.

Arians might have made the dumbest call in Alabama history. But at least Alabama was leading when he made the call, leading at Auburn, not trailing by 36 points at Arkansas, where fans barely had time to clean up from the week-long party celebrating a victory over SMU and get ready for the nationally ranked Tide.

Oh, yeah, Mike DuBose has turned this program around. Kind of the same way the captain of the Titanic turned his ship around after hitting the first iceberg.

You might call this movie "TideTanic".

Some people will say it is too early to hit the panic button. Wrong. It was hit so many times Saturday night the button is already worn out.

Losing 42-6 against Arkansas was not a disaster. Nope. It was eight months of goodwill being sucked out the way air goes out a shattered window in a 747 at 38,000 feet.

All of the goodwill, all of those warm fuzzies and screams of "Roll Tide" now are scattered over some parts of Arkansas.

But at least DuBose said after the game he is not going to change anything. Absolutely not. Forget about it. Let's stick with the same plan against Florida. Can you say 84-6?

Now I know how Hillary Rodham Clinton felt.

Now I know what it is like to believe in someone for eight months and have it all shred apart, like a junkyard dog tearing into a fresh piece of meat.

I was just beginning to believe DuBose had everything on the right page. I thought progress had been made. I thought things were moving in the right direction.

Oh, sure, some people will say take a look around the nation, all is not lost. Look at Washington getting bounced by Nebraska by seven touchdowns.

That is Nebraska, for heaven's sake. Arkansas might go to a bowl game this year. But I can tell you right now, it will not be the Fiesta Bowl.

With Florida coming to town, you will hear a lot this week about the most recent regular-season game against the Gators.

Yada, yada, yada. Florida wins 35-0 in 1991 and Alabama does not lose another game for two seasons.

Well, forget that idiotic theory.

Alabama is going to lose again this Saturday. Oh, it will not be that bad, because Florida could care less about playing Alabama. The Gators already are thinking about the following week, when they can take out frustration and revenge on LSU for last year's shocker on the Bayou.

Oh, the Gators will show up Saturday in Tuscaloosa. And, of course, they will go through the motions.

As for Alabama, it should be an interesting week to listen to DuBose telling Crimson Tide fans not to lose faith. It will be interesting to hear him say what happened in Arkansas was only one game. Nothing more. Perhaps DuBose will be speaking the truth. Perhaps this night of infamy was only a small blip on the radar screen.

Or perhaps this 36-point loss, the most shameful night of football for Alabama in 41 years, is a harbinger of things to come under DuBose.

So in the end, one must ask what really happened? What was the difference between Arkansas and Alabama, two schools that ended 1997 with same 4-7 record.

Arkansas hired a fresh face and woke up a sleeping giant. Alabama has hired a dull face and put a giant to sleep.

TRUE AUBURN FANS WILL SIDE WITH HOUSEL

October 26, 1998

AUBURN – On a glorious autumn afternoon, the loudest noise made Saturday at Jordan-Hare Stadium was the sound of silence.

Auburn fans cheered occasionally for their football team against Louisiana Tech. Mostly, though, they there quiet, wondering now whom to believe in the volcanic aftermath of Terry Bowden's resignation.

Should they side with the people who run the athletic department or the martyr who fell from grace?

They have been fed gossip and rumor from the FOB: Friends of Bowden. They have been told Athletic Director David Housel was out to get the former head coach. They have been told Robert E. Lowder, the school's most prominent trustee and the one who brought Bowden to Auburn in the first place, got mad and ordered his head cut off in a huff.

Amazingly, many good Auburn fans, those who bleed orange and blue, are falling for this sack of horse feathers.

They believe Bowden was good and Housel and Lowder are evil. They believe a man like Housel, who has given his life to Auburn and Lowder, who in addition to his time and effort, to say nothing of millions of dollars, could be wrong about this situation.

The FOB point to Bowden's overall record but ignore the most recent and troubling trend. In unison, the FOB talk about how terrible these men are to even consider letting a coach go with a 1-5 record. Of course, the FOB conveniently have forgotten the truth of the matter.

We know about 20-0. We know about the Southeastern Conference championship game experience last year. We know because Bowden told us so many times.

But we never heard Bowden talk about the 16 games since this point in 1994 when he faced teams ranked in the AP Top 25. Well, the record was 4-12. Or the fact that the school lost five times to unranked schools while Auburn was ranked.

Do the FOB mention their fallen leader lost five of his last six home games? Or what about the 18-15-1 record since the mid-point of 1994 against SEC schools?

So do you think Housel and Lowder are blind? Or is it possible they saw a trend developing that might be irreversible and showed concern?

Well, why, you ask, did they award Bowden with this infamous seven-year contract? Well, as we all know now, it wasn't really a seven-year contract. That was a lot of nonsense that Bowden wanted in the agreement to make him look good, to say nothing of assuage his massive ego. I don't know why Housel went along with the deal. Yet, he did, perhaps overreacting to criticism.

Remember who was screaming bloody murder about getting a new agreement. It was Bowden. He put Housel on the spot. Finally, the athletic director gave him what he wanted. Obviously, it came with a price tag.

When Bowden went into Housel's office Wednesday morning asking for a vote of confidence, he didn't get one.

Instead of doing what he was being paid to do, at a price tag of nearly $1 million per year, Bowden tucked his tail and threatened to quit. Bowden got involved in a high stakes game of poker with Housel, and when the athletic director didn't call his bluff, the contest was over.

Bowden was out the door.

After telling his coaching staff and his players, to say nothing of his loyal fans days earlier, that he would fight through the labyrinth, Bowden walked away.

Remarkably, good Auburn fans are buying his side of the story versus the word of people like Housel and Lowder.

On a personal note, I know all three people involved very

well. I'll try to put this in the most tactful way possible. But if I had to stake my life on something Bowden told me against something uttered to me by Housel or Lowder, the choice would be simple.

You can't always judge a man by the company he keeps. But in this case, I'll sure take my chances.

Instead of assailing these two men for having too much power to overthrow a football coach, which is the story according to the FOB, I would credit them for being sagacious. I would compliment them for looking at the entire picture and not only the won-lost record.

Bill Curry had a solid record at Alabama. However, in the process, he was running the program into the ground.

Tennessee fans reacted with outrage and enmity six years ago when the school replaced Johnny Majors with Phillip Fulmer. Majors had a good record. He had won three SEC championships. However, officials didn't like the direction he was taking the program. They felt he was out of control and attempted to stop the bleeding before it was too late.

The program received a black eye, much like Auburn is getting now around the nation. But what happened and where is Tennessee today? The Vols are undefeated, ranked No. 3 in the nation and have just beaten Alabama for the fourth consecutive time.

Auburn could use a black eye like that.

The easy way out for Housel would have been to ignore the rivulet of rumors coming out of the Auburn football complex. It would have been easy to look the other way and turn the other cheek at the severe discipline problems on this football team. Why worry about the increasingly large number of thugs Bowden was bringing into the program out of desperation, the ruckus some of these players were causing on campus and around town on a steady basis?

Why worry that some of Bowden's players laughed and made fun of him behind his back? Why worry that some of his own coaches did the same thing?

Why worry that Bill Oliver indicated to friends this was going to be his last year of putting up with Bowden's nonsense?

If you are Housel, you say, no big deal. Business as usual. Bad year. It will get better. After all, Bowden once won 20 consecutive games.

Why be concerned about a paranoid coach who thinks the world is out to get him, who thinks people are bugging his phone conversations, who believes private investigators are trailing him?

That's just normal behavior for a successful head football coach.

Right.

If you are Housel, you ignore all of this, and when Bowden shows up in your office on Wednesday morning, you look him in the eye and say: "Terry, don't you worry about a thing. You continue to run this program into the ground and we don't care. Lose them all this year. Lose them all next year. Keep recruiting the same way you are. Because it doesn't matter.

"You won your first 20 games. Your Daddy is Bobby Bowden. And we here at Auburn are a bunch of ignorant, primeval, tobacco-chewing rednecks who are eternally grateful for the day you ever graced us with your presence."

Or, as what really happened, you look Bowden square in the eye and say, "We'll address this when the season is over."

Did Bowden do what any man would do? Go back to work and prove he could still coach? Prove he was worth the ridiculous sum of money he was being paid?

Or did he throw a tantrum, act like a petulant child, threaten revenge and offer his resignation on the spot?

When you are choosing sides on whom to believe in the roaring controversy engulfing the Loveliest Village on the Plains, take a deep breath and look at the big picture. Use common sense.

Do you believe in Housel, a good and decent man, who has devoted a lifetime to making Auburn University a better place? Or do you believe in Bowden, whose love for himself always has out-weighed his feelings for Auburn and practically everything else?

Tough choice, huh?

TUBERVILLE THE RIGHT CHOICE TO RESTORE AUBURN'S PRIDE

November 28, 1998

In selecting Thomas Hawley Tuberville as Auburn's new foot-ball coach, athletic director David Housel passed on the easiest choice (Pat Sullivan) or the most popular choice (Bill Oliver).

Instead, he has made the best choice.

Housel has found a man strong enough to lead but charis-matic enough to unite. He has found a man who pulled Ole Miss out of a raging inferno. He has found a man who brought self-respect back to a pounded and pummeled campus and made the Rebels competitive again, in spite of a virulent assault on the pro-gram by the NCAA.

Some will say his inability to beat Alabama and Auburn is a black mark to be held against him. Say what you want. However, when you consider the amount of money and support funneled into those two respective programs, in relation to Ole Miss, wiser heads will prevail.

Tuberville has never been able to coach with a full compli-ment of players. He has always had one hand tied behind his back at Ole Miss. It will be a different story at Auburn.

His biggest predicament at Auburn will be in bringing college football's most dysfunctional family back together again. It won't be easy. However, something tells me Tuberville can do the job.

If Terry Bowden, perhaps, the most narcissistic human being

to ever step foot in Lee County, could become a cult figure among Auburn fans, Tuberville will have no problem whatsoever.

Some say Bowden's biggest mistake was starting out 11-0. Considering the schedule next year has pit stops in Tallahassee, FL, Baton Rouge, LA, Knoxville, TN, Fayetteville, AR, and Athens, GA, I think a winning season might be a more pragmatic goal for Auburn fans.

Even that could be a stretch.

No one can predict the future. However, from what I know of this 44-year-old coaching nova, Auburn fans won't be embarrassed by his actions. The program won't be the subject of gossip and rumors.

The program might not compete for a BCS berth right away. However, with Tuberville, neither will the program be the laughingstock of the nation, the subject of sarcasm and scorn, the longest running soap opera in the sport.

Many have blamed the likes of Housel and powerful trustee Bobby Lowder for running Bowden out of town. In truth, Bowden ran himself out on a rail, by doing a wretched job of recruiting and a pathetic job of coaching.

He tucked his tail and bolted after a 1-5 start. He wanted someone else to get the blame for a 3-8 record. Bowden was tantamount to a one-hit wonder in rock music. After his first hit record, the rest of the songs seemed to pale in comparison.

Ole Miss fans were in love with Tuberville, but some grew weary of his yearly dalliances with other schools. Tuberville turned Arkansas down a year ago because he didn't feel right about the situation.

The only way Bowden's name ever got mentioned for a job occurred when one of his publicity department flacks ran it up the flagpole with media cronies. The rumors didn't last long because they weren't true.

Whether this is Tuberville's last stop as a coach remains to be seen. However, I don't think Tuberville will be searching the classified ads for coaching jobs, with the amount of money being paid to him and with the state-of-the art facilities Auburn has to offer.

There is old saying in politics that one can best gauge a national candidate or issue by how it plays in Peoria. In state football parlance, how an Auburn coach plays in Tuscaloosa is perhaps the best indicator.

Folks in Tuscaloosa were privately pulling for Brother Oliver to get the job. They knew his clock would be cleaned in recruiting. They are not so sure about Tuberville, who has a reputation as a skilled recruiter.

The last few months have been among the worst in modern Auburn history. And that's saying something. However, it's worth remembering Auburn has been down before. Pat Dye came to town in 1981 and restored pride and promise to the program.

Bowden lifted their spirits again after the Eric Ramsey affair. However, it was a quick fix, a house of cards that soon collapsed. The new coach is not a Band-Aid. He is not a short-term solution. He is the real deal.

In hiring Tommy Tuberville, David Housel has made both a bold and brilliant choice for Auburn's future.

THIS DATE STILL FROZEN IN TIME

January 27, 1999

Shortly after lunch Tuesday afternoon, I noticed the date on the front page of the newspaper: January 26. It was about the same time, too, approximately 1:30 p.m.

Time stopped for a moment. The sunshine froze and the wind became still.

In my mind, the calendar flipped back 16 years - to the

moment Paul "Bear" Bryant passed away.

There is no magical number connected to 16 years. Usually, those outside the family note an anniversary in terms of 10, 20 or 50 years.

However, on the next anniversary of Bryant's death, the calendar will read 2000. There's something strange about that.

Where were you when you heard the news? Where were you when you heard that the greatest college football coach in history had died? Where were you when the world, at least in the state of Alabama, seemed to come to a halt?

I was at Legion Field covering a practice for the Birmingham Stallions of the USFL. Someone ran up and said: "Hey, Coach Bryant died."

There had been a short item in the newspaper in the morning about him being in the hospital. But nobody thought it was serious.

I grabbed a quarter, dialed the newspaper's number and confirmed the news.

Ten minutes later, back at the paper, it was like a scene from Armageddon. People running in every direction. Having to react without emotion. Being a newspaperman is just like being a doctor - except our W-2 form at the end of the year usually has one less digit.

I sat down and started writing and didn't stop until dusk.

The first thing that came into my head was an event four weeks earlier, when Bryant had invited a small group of writers into his suite, on the day of his final game at the Liberty Bowl.

Bryant shook hands with every man in the room and posed for a picture. Afterward, he stopped and said softly: "I wonder what I'll be doing a year from today."

Less than a month later, he was dead.

The next three days were unlike anything this state has ever seen. The next day, after visiting his casket at the Hayes Funeral Home, I dropped by his office in Coleman Coliseum.

Linda Knowles, his secretary, was at her desk, fighting back tears as she helped to make arrangements.

While I talked to her, a letter arrived from a retired military man, addressed to Coach Bryant. There were still messages in his box.

I looked at his office and asked Knowles if she had been inside.

"Yes, I've been in there since he died," she said, with tears welling in her eyes. "When I go in there, it's just like he's on a trip."

His final days were happy ones, she said.

Bryant answered mail. One day, he went and hit golf balls at the local club. He chewed on bologna and cheese or had soup for lunch. He always drank Countrytime Lemonade.

Two days before his death, he was in Birmingham on business, speaking to a sponsor's dinner. On Tuesday, Jan. 25, he came into his office at noon and spent most of the day on the phone.

Bryant also visited with former quarterback Steadman Shealy. He left at 4:30 p.m. and stopped at the home of close friend Jimmy Hinton for a visit. He began suffering chest pains. He went to the hospital from there.

On his final morning, Bryant called friends from the hospital, trying to help assistants get jobs. He also bought an expensive bond from his stock broker in Birmingham. At 12:30 p.m., he was struck with a massive heart attack.

The funeral was unlike anything this state had ever seen.

In looking back, it wasn't the luminaries that I remembered best, people such as Joe Namath and Woody Hayes, Eddie Robinson and Governor George Wallace.

It was the small little girl, rubbing her eyes, fighting back tears. It was the state trooper, standing still, his hat over his heart. People who didn't even know each other, holding hands and crying together.

Finebaum Said...

It was the group of small children sitting on a porch in front of a church near Bryant Denny Stadium, behind a sign in a roped off area, saying: "Reserved for Little Friends."

It was the little people who came out by the hundreds of thousands on that crisp Friday morning 16 years ago. The ones who had never met the man, who only knew him from the last row in the end zone or on the television screen or through the crackling sound of a warped radio.

It was the little kid with the sign: "God Needed An Offensive Coordinator" that touched so many. It was the construction workers standing over the interstate, their hard hats doffed in respect.

It was the feeling that day that no matter what happened in the future, this state would never be the same again without Paul "Bear" Bryant.

John Forney, the legendary announcer, summed up the week and the memorable funeral best, in his book, "Above The Noise Of The Crowd."

He wrote: "The ministers were properly brief. As I looked at the casket and the youthful player pallbearers, I thought sadly that his strength and power and force were now still. And I hoped there would be others possessing these qualities when the country needed them. He was a hell of a man.

"The service was over, and I walked with the crowd out through the iron gates of Elmwood. It was journey's end."

REMEMBER LEWIS EACH AS A PROFILE IN COURAGE

February 13, 1999

He won't be there tonight.

He won't be there in the overflow crowd that will gather in Coleman Coliseum when No. 2 Georgia meets No. 1 Alabama in women's gymnastics. He won't experience the thunderous ovation. He'll miss the light show. He won't hear the music.

You see, the biggest fan of Alabama gymnastics died a few months ago at the age of 24. You might have read a line or two in the newspaper about Lewis Each. Perhaps you even might have seen or heard a comment on radio and television.

Lew deserved much more than that.

This was a young man who deserved books written about his life and movies made about his valor. His story should be required reading for every child in Alabama's school system.

Lew had cystic fibrosis. His final years were a struggle, often painful and difficult to watch. Yet, it also was a brilliant profile in courage that inspired everyone around him.

He wrote for the *Crimson and White* in Tuscaloosa. He was a correspondent for *The Birmingham News*. For the *Birmingham Post Herald*, he once wrote a guest column in this space.

He never looked back, although he knew looking forward was fruitless.

Only one time did Lew tell me he regretted something.

Last year, Mitch Albom, a gifted sportswriter in Detroit, wrote a book on his former college professor, dying of Lou Gehrig's Disease, entitled, "Tuesdays with Morrie."

It is still No. 1 on the best-seller list, 70 weeks after being published.

"We blew it," Lew told me late one night from his hospital

room where he spent most of his final year.

"Blew what?" I asked

"We should have done this book We would have made a fortune."

And he was right. Who else could joke about something like that? Who else could joke about doing a book about their own death?

Lew had so many friends in high places that it became comical. Once when I was visiting him at the hospital, the phone rang. He nodded his head a couple of times, seemingly bored with the conversation.

I thought perhaps the hospital kitchen had called and inquired if he wanted to change his breakfast order from Corn Flakes to Froot Loops.

"Who was that?" I asked.

"Oh, that was Coach Stallings calling from Texas."

A year ago, I dropped by the hospital right after Mike DuBose had fired four assistant coaches in the aftermath of the Iron Bowl loss. He was putting up the phone as I entered the room.

"I just talked to Coach DuBose," Lew was saying.

"What did he say?" I asked.

"Not much. I cut it off pretty quickly. Considering what he had done to those four coaches, I was afraid he might fire me if the conversation went too long."

Not long before he died, Lewis and I met for dinner at a Chinese restaurant.

I was in a hurry.

Naturally, Lew was not.

He took 10 minutes from the car into the restaurant with his oxygen pack. I was ordering before the waitress had dropped the water glass and egg rolls. Lew was memorizing the menu. I have never seen such a frail person enjoy food more than Lew did on that night. He chewed every bite, savoring the flavor and taste.

I was rambling in mid-sentence when Lew stopped me. "You know I'm running out of time," he said looking straight at me.

What do you say at a moment like this? What do you say to someone who has just informed you that he is close to death?

I nodded my head. What else could I do?

Through it all, one person's devotion was unwavering - Sarah Patterson, Alabama's gymnastics coach.

Whenever another medical crisis arose, she would race to Birmingham to spend time with him. Even when she was dealing with another crisis -her husband's bout with cancer- Patterson was there for Lewis.

Patterson dedicated this year's media guide to Lew with a poignant picture of him sitting at press row and a quotation from him:

"Everybody has the same 24 hours in a day. No one gets any in advance. You do what you want with yours. I'm going to use mine."

Patterson also made sure -with the help of University of Alabama President Andrew Sorensen and Dean of Communications Cully Clark- that Lew received his degree posthumously in December.

Coach Patterson held the arms of Lew's parents, Jean and Winston Each, as they stood in for him at graduation. Everyone in the place stood and cheered as the three walked down the aisle. There wasn't a dry eye in the building.

So tonight, when the music is blaring and the joint is jumping in Coleman Coliseum, stop for just a moment and think about the person who isn't there. Think about Lewis Each.

He won't be there tonight.

At least not where we can see him.

POLLY DUBOSE STANDS BY HER MAN

May 8, 1999

TUSCALOOSA - On the outside, she was beaming. But deep down, on the inside of her body and soul, one had to wonder what feelings, what emotions must be going on right now.

"Come on in," the slender, attractive woman said as she motioned me into the house early Friday morning. "I hope you didn't have any trouble finding the place."

On this glorious spring day, the only sound that could be heard was of birds chirping in a nearby cluster of trees and an occasional grinding sound of equipment coming from construction workers in the distance.

The newspaper was still laying unopened in the cul de sac in this town's newest and swankiest real-estate development.

On the drive to the house through the nestled woods, one spotted former Alabama Athletic Director Hootie Ingram, dressed in shorts, watering the grass.

This beautiful red brick home with three white columns in front is the residence of the First Family of Alabama football: Mike and Polly DuBose.

"This has been quite a week," Mrs. DuBose said as she fetched her guest a cup of coffee. "It has just been so hard on everyone."

Dressed casually in a blue jeans jumper and wearing a cross around her neck, she looked considerably younger than her 45 years.

"We go to bed early and get up about 5," she said. Her husband had left earlier to play in a charity golf tournament at a nearby club.

Polly DuBose looked a tad tired, which perhaps is understandable, considering her husband of almost 24 years has spend the majority of the week denying rumors of an inappropriate relationship with his secretary.

As she walked her guest to an outside deck, which overlooks Lake Tuscaloosa, the sounds of Christian music could be heard faintly in the background.

"I just really don't know what to say," she said.

Polly DuBose began by telling the story of her courtship with her husband. They met in Opp.

"Actually, you don't meet someone in Opp, since everyone knows everyone else," she said, laughing.

Mike and Polly DuBose were high school sweethearts.

"I know this sounds corny, but our first date was to church," she said. "There wasn't much else to do in Opp."

Mike played football. Polly was a cheerleader. They dated and broke up. They made up and broke up again. Finally, she married him during the end of her senior year at Alabama.

She proudly points out her husband is a year older.

As I sit listening to her talk of her deep religious faith, of her blissfully happy marriage, of the close bond with her family, I wonder what I am doing here in her house. I wonder about the volatile events of this week.

Polly DuBose talks for a long time about her Christian faith. Most of her free time, she said, is spent speaking to church groups.

The subject turns to the difficulty of being in the spotlight. She relates a story about her daughter, Julie (who is now 22), being booed on a school bus while they lived in Tampa when Mike worked for the local NFL team.

She talked about losing her father two years ago to cancer.

"He loved Mike so much and was so proud of him getting the job here," she said. "And he died one month before his first game."

DuBose's first year was a tough time for everyone. The Tide finished 4-7 and some Alabama were fans were hoping DuBose wouldn't make it back for the second year.

"One of the hardest things we've ever been through," she

said.

After the losing season, which ended with the controversial and calamitous Iron Bowl (remember when DuBose said he didn't know the play called at the end of the game?), things turned ugly for the family.

The DuBoses were at a high school baseball playoff game last year watching son Michael, 18, who has signed a scholarship to play at Alabama.

The announcer introduced him and gave out his number. However, fans in the stands began chanting, "4 and 7. ... 4 and 7."

Later, the umpire had to briefly stop the game, because fans were harassing Michael in the outfield.

"We really found out who our friends were after that," she said. "My husband and I grieved over letting so many people down that year. I wondered if it was really worth it."

They decided it was.

Polly DuBose said her Christian faith helped her through the darkest days. However, just when things seemed to be calming down last year, another tragedy struck.

One year ago this weekend, Mike's younger sister, Renee, died of Lupus. She was 40. The DuBose family will spend this Mother's Day weekend in Opp to commemorate the sad anniversary.

"That was so hard for him," Polly DuBose said, tears welling in her eyes.

Finally, the subject turned to the rumors. She talked about the toll on her children, of what they all have been through during this nightmarish week.

"I believe in Mike deeply," she said. "I don't believe the rumors. There is no truth to them at all. Not a shred. When I first heard it, I couldn't believe they were talking about my husband. He's always been an honest man. He has always told the truth."

Polly DuBose also strongly agrees with the debatable decision for the Alabama coach to go public with his denial.

"This was a person attacking his family, and he had to

respond," she said.

She declined to speculate publicly on why someone would want to spread such malicious gossip. She shrugged her shoulders, saying: "I just know how much this has hurt Mike."

Despite the pain this week, I was struck by Polly DuBose's remarkable outlook on this unfortunate situation.

"There are brighter days ahead," she said. "There is so much to excited about in the future."

She talked of the upcoming football season. She mentioned her daughter's approaching graduation in a few months from college and her son about to enter Alabama.

She reminded me of something her husband said the day he was hired to replace Gene Stallings as Alabama's head football coach:

"Dreams do come true and prayer works."

The conversation was drawing to a close. It had been difficult for Polly DuBose to talk about this subject. However, at every fork in the conversation, she seemed to find a light, a testament to get through the exhausting and painful answers.

Her last comment seemed to unlock that mystery.

"When you have faith in the Lord," Polly DuBose said, "He meets your every need."

CYBER PAUL WEIGHS IN ON CHAT ROOMS

May 15, 1999

The hottest thing on the Internet these days -that is, other than spreading rumors trying to ruin people's lives- are chat rooms.

This is when someone well-known or is supposedly an expert answers questions from anonymous people with stupid, idiotic names, who obviously have nothing better to do with their lives.

I think even my garbage man has been featured on a chat site. But not me.

Until now.

Since no one will invite me, I'm going to have one right here in the newspaper. For those who have never been online to witness a guest chat, take a look.

Chat Host: Welcome to the Paul Finebaum guest chat. Please refrain from using vulgarity or making threats. As you know, Mr. Finebaum writes for the *Birmingham Post Herald* and has been at times vicious, arrogant, rude, capricious, thoughtless, vindicative, unfair or totally off-base. Sometimes, he's all of these things in one column. And these are his good points.

Bama Bubba: Hey, what do you think of Alabama's athletic director?

Finebaum: I think Hootie Ingram has done a great job for the University of Alabama.

Puff Daddy: What's your take on Robert Baker going pro?

Finebaum: First of all, a lucky break for Tuberville. But the most interesting thing is he signed with Ricky Davis, who is Terry Bowden's attorney.

Tator Tot: Do you think Bowden will ever coach again?

Finebaum: Nope. Or, at least, not for a while. I don't think a reputable school would want him around after the way he handled the Auburn situation. Bowden should do well, though at ABC Sports (he'll be in the studio for college football). He could always moonlight as Tatoo's understudy in the remake of "Fantasy Island."

BlazerDog: Why do you hate UAB?

Finebaum: I don't. When their football team draws more than 10,000 a game and the basketball program averages more than what they get at a Vestavia Hills High School baseball game, give me a call. Until then, don't bother me.

Big Al: What teams do you like in the SEC East and West?

Finebaum: I like Florida in the East although Tennessee fans maintain they have the best team ever coming back. In the West, I like Alabama, although just about every school in the league - with the exception of Auburn- probably has a chance.

GatorHater: Why are you always sucking up to Steve Spurrier?

Finebaum: Because he's the best coach in the history of the SEC.

TideHoops: Do you think Alabama will go the NCAA basketball tournament next year?

Finebaum: Yes. Mark Gottfried, who I think is one of the best young coaches in the country, will not only get Alabama to the NCAA next year, but will have the Tide in the Final Four sometime in the next few years.

GatorHater: Hey, you idiot, are you insinuating Spurrier is better than Bear Bryant?

Finebaum: Oh, did I say that? What I meant to say he is the best coach since Bryant, although, he would have given Bear a run for his money.

Sweet Dome Alabama: Will Birmingham ever get a dome?

Finebaum: I think so. There is a lot of chatter behind the scenes about a new dome proposal. Also, I think the arrival of Honda in Alabama could play a big factor. The American Honda Company is one of the biggest sports advertisers in the country and likes to be involved in the local community.

The Big Dogs: Do you think DuBose will last at Alabama?

Finebaum: Well, one would think DuBose will last awhile, since he's won three consecutive national championships in recruiting.

Green and Gold: How long do you think it will take UAB football to be taken seriously?

Finebaum: Won't happen. Playing in C-USA will help short-term. But I don't think UAB will even have football in 15 years.

Chat Host: OK, we can take a few more questions before Mr. Finebaum has to leave.

Toomer's Corner: Is it true that your parents abandoned you as a child and you were raised by a pack of wolves?

Chat Host: Umm. Two more and let's keep it clean.

GoVols: I've seen your picture and I just have one question about your college days at Tennessee: Have you ever worn a jock strap at Neyland Stadium?

Finebaum: No, I couldn't find one to fit.

RC and Moon Pie: Why do you hate auto racing so much?

Finebaum: Well, I really don't. I think the folks that run NASCAR are the best sports marketers in the world, with the possible exception of the WWF. However, let me share a story on racing, which I read in *Sports Illustrated* about a writer's one and only journey to a track. He wrote: "Race fans, I had inferred from my one visit, fell into one of two categories -tattooed, shirtless, sewer-mouthed drunks- and their husbands."

TALLAHASSEE HOT SPOTS ARE FEW

June 2, 1999

Poor Hal Baird. The man can't seem to win even when he is winning.

Last week, the headlines about BrotherGate overshadowed Auburn playing host to its first NCAA baseball regional in ages. This week, the showdown in the Super Regional will be eclipsed by talk about the Auburn-FSU football series being cancelled and Auburn's feud with the Bowden boys.

What's a man to do?

Well, let me try to help. I know the Tigers will be anxious during their trip to Tallahassee, FL. So as a master traveler, let me suggest a few places of interest for Baird and the Auburn baseball team during the weekend trip.

As most of you know, Tallahassee is the capital of Florida, even though the rest of the state is embarrassed to claim the city.

One thing is certain: In the event of a World War (heaven forbid), I'm heading straight to Tallahassee. Enemy pilots would take one look below and conclude someone already has dropped the big one.

This is the home of a university that said it wanted to join the Atlantic Coast Conference over the Southeastern Conference to elevate its basketball program. During December, the best place in town to get away from the Christmas rush is the Leon County Civic Center, where FSU plays its home games, because it is empty other than the two teams.

I checked with the Tallahassee Visitor's Guide on Tuesday morning for hot spots to visit during the NCAA baseball tournament. A nice young man named Christopher answered the phone on the first ring (he might have an easier job than the Maytag repairman).

I mentioned the prospects of a visit to Tallahassee. "What

should I see?" I asked.

"Ummm," Christopher said, seemingly stumped for a moment. "Well, uh ... umm ... we have museums ... all different kinds of parks. ..."

"Really," I said, "is that it?"

"Well," he continued, "you could come by here. We are located right across the street from the capitol. We would be happy to give you a brochure."

Can you imagine the same response had I called the Visitor's Bureau in Orlando, FL, or Tampa, FL., or Miami? Do you think they would be fumbling for an answer? I would be on the phone 30 minutes just trying to decide between Walt Disney World or Epcot or Universal Studios or MGM or a trip to Busch Gardens.

Well, anyway, since a man who is paid (probably $3 bucks per hour) to help visitors in Tallahassee couldn't do the job, I have decided to chip in and help the Auburn team myself.

Here are few places of interest for the upcoming visit: For starters, the Tigers (they might have to call Terry Bowden for some help) could drop by the FSU football complex between 12:30-1:30 p.m. and watch Bobby Bowden take his daily nap. Just as they warn you at the zoo not to feed the animals, beware of talking to him right after the nap. Old Man Bowden is grumpy and grouchy. In an hour, Bowden usually has calmed down and is studying plays, since he no longer seems to remember them during games.

Leon County Jail. This is a site where most of FSU's best players have been booked, finger printed and had their mug shots taken. There are statues of the players (in full prison garb) at the museum, with the particular crime listed in front and the punishment levied out by Bobby Bowden underneath. Don't bother bringing your reading glasses for that. There is a gift shop where you can buy FSU jerseys with both the player's real number and prison number listed. Also, a booklet, "How to beat a rape charge," co-authored by the 1993 national championship team, is for sale. You also can buy the Florida State joke book. However,

Finebaum Said...

the biggest joke in FSU history is the national championship in 1993. Here is a team that lost to Notre Dame but still beat out the Irish for the title, because it was payback to Bowden from all of his coaching and sportswriting friends.

Luden's Cough Drops Exhibition Honoring FSU Football. For a small fee, you can sit back and enjoy the greatest choke jobs in FSU football history. One can start with the most recent: The Fiesta Bowl loss to Tennessee for the national championship. Or, one could turn the clock back to 1997 and watch Florida's 52-20 pounding of the Seminoles in the Sugar Bowl. Or take your pick of the year when an FSU missed field-goal attempt against Miami ended up costing the home boys a shot at the national title. Of course, don't forget the final game in 1997 against the Gators when the Seminoles were undefeated and headed toward the national title when Florida burned the defense in the waning moments, 32-29.

You also can see a display of former FSU player Burt Reynolds' greatest movies (one) and his biggest flops (the past 34 he has done).

Also, a cutout of FSU's biggest goofball graduate, ESPN commentator Lee Corso, is on exhibit.

The campus Foot Locker store. Just put on an FSU jersey and walk out with all the free shoes you can stick in your pockets and under your shirt.

CAN'T LIE LOW...
COACH SHOULD RESIGN

August 7, 1999

In a society crazed by political correctness, should a person -who is arguably the state's best-known figure- remain in his position after admitting he lied to his wife, his family, his friends, his coaching staff and the people who write him the check for $500,000 about an affair with his secretary?

These are just a couple of the questions raging through the state this weekend in the wake of the shattering events concerning Alabama football coach Mike DuBose.

First, let's take a deep breath and examine the damage scattered across the Crimson Empire. Let us begin with his wife and family.

I assume DuBose lied about the affair to his wife, Polly. I assume this because I sat in her kitchen two days after the initial rumor surfaced in May. For approximately two hours, I listened to Mrs. DuBose passionately defend her husband and say she believed in him. Tears welled in her eyes and deep emotion was etched across her brow.

If she was lying to me, it was the greatest theatrical performance in the history of the world. I don't think it was.

We don't have to assume DuBose lied to Alabama staffers and administrators. We know he did. This man who often talks about morality and integrity looked decade-long friends squarely in the eye and lied his rear end off.

Interestingly, Alabama insiders maintain DuBose was furious at one assistant coach in particular, privately blaming this man for spreading malicious gossip about the affair in an effort to help land the head coaching position - at least, on an interim basis. So while DuBose is blaming one of his assistant coaches, in the process, he is living a lie.

Of course, it caught up with him.

In the aftermath of DuBose's denial, there were rumors making the rounds a payoff was in the works. Meanwhile, DuBose traveled across the state, shrugging off the rumors like a bad cold, talking about how he had brought Alabama back from the wilderness and how the program was on the verge of something special.

Meanwhile, those who dared to even discuss the rumors and innuendo were vilified by the Alabama family and by a group of self-righteous cads in the news media.

So now what?

Can DuBose survive? Can he right the ship? Can this man who lied to his coaching staff now somehow keep the same group of people together? Hardly.

These people have mortgages to pay and mouths to feed. How is DuBose going to be able to convince these people he will be at Alabama much longer, now that his contract has been slashed?

What will his players think? Oh, they will say the right things for the cameras. But one can bet they will be cracking on the head coach behind closed doors. I can't wait for the first player to get punished by DuBose for failing to tell the truth.

The Alabama family will say the right things in defense of DuBose. But they are not behind him. Privately, most Alabama fans I have talked to are embarrassed, if not humiliated by his actions.

They are humiliated in part because DuBose's stupidity has now given Auburn a chance to return the volleys and jokes they have suffered for months. Within an hour of DuBose's Tuscaloosa press conference Thursday, I stood talking with Auburn football coach Tommy Tuberville in Mobile. We were among several speakers at a charity banquet hosted by ESPN commentator Mike Gottfried and Tuberville's silence on the matter was deafening.

However, one can only imagine the noise raised on the

recruiting trails this winter if DuBose remains at Alabama. By stripping his contract down to three years, the Alabama administration has killed recruiting for the coming year.

Here is a man who got on his high horse a few days ago, talking about Travis Carroll and Eric Locke, saying they made commitments to the university when they signed a scholarship and would not be released. Meanwhile, the same man is lying to the most important people in his life while carrying on with a subordinate - of all things.

In the end, Mike DuBose lied a few months ago to save his job. It's possible had he told the truth, by now, this would have been an old story. It's also possible he might have been replaced, relegated to hosting a local talk radio show with Wimp Sanderson. They certainly have a few things in common.

If he lied to save his job over an affair with a secretary, can DuBose be believed on other matters? Realizing now the only possible way he can save his job is by winning and winning big, will other issues be compromised to save his career?

Unfortunately, DuBose has become a liability to the University of Alabama. In time, and with a lot of luck, it's possible he could turn the tide.

Yet, it's a long shot.

A departure for DuBose now would be painful for all sides. However, considering the circumstances, it would be in Alabama's best interest to let him go.

BEAR WOULDN'T LIKE THIS MESS

September 25, 1999

The sun had just slipped behind the western horizon, bringing an end to a lustrous late summer day. Driving past rows of gravestones on the small rocky road, I arrived at Lot 57, Block 30, right under a tall hickory tree.

As I walked slowly toward the familiar marker, the tranquility was interrupted with white hot flashes of lightning crashing from the sky. The ground shook for a moment. Then, the voice was heard.

"So you are back?"

It was the deep, resonant voice of the Bear.

"Yes sir, Coach," I said. "I couldn't wait any longer. I needed to fill you in on recent events."

Before the 1998 season, I had been here to Elmwood, giving Coach Paul "Bear" Bryant an update following Alabama's 4-7 record. Bryant had not followed Alabama football in some time. He said he had given up on the Tide after the hiring of Bill Curry. Briefly, he went back to Alabama during the 1992 season when Gene "Bebes" Stallings won the national title. However, in recent years, Bryant had bought a Florida Gator snoot and was a card-carrying Steve Spurrier fan.

"So, what's the latest?" he said.

"Well, they fired Bob Bockrath this week," I told him.

"Good move," Bryant said. "He was the guy who didn't even know I went to school at Alabama?"

"That's right, coach."

"Well, I assume they either gave the job to Lee Roy or Bebes or Mal Moore," Bryant said.

I informed Bryant that Andrew Sorensen, the school president, was conducting a nationwide search and made it clear that Alabama ties were not a prerequisite.

"Well, that little bow-tied son of a buck doesn't run the school," Bryant said.

"Well, sir, he does right now."

"Well, what does Paul Jr. have to say?"

I informed Bryant that his son and the school president weren't exactly dove-hunting buddies.

"Well, how's old DuBose doing as coach?"

"Fans are down on him right now, Coach. He was going for three in a row last week and the team lost."

"Well, I can't say I'm happy," Bryant said. "It's tough nowadays with those stupid scholarship limitations. But I had trouble winning three national championships in a row, too."

"Excuse me, Coach," I said, nervously, "but DuBose was trying to win three straight games for the first time, not three straight national championships."

"Who beat them? Don't tell me. Those little ... from Notre Dame or Penn State, right? Never should've even put them Yankee boys on the schedule."

"No sir, Coach. Louisiana Tech. It was the second time DuBose has lost to La. Tech in three years."

Bryant groaned loudly. The ground seemed to move for a moment as another bolt of lightning crashed down, nearly striking me.

"Well, other than that, is old DuBose doing a good job?" Bryant asked.

"No sir. He almost got fired last summer for having an improper relationship with his secretary."

The ground shook again. I listened closely and I swore I heard Coach Bryant cackling.

"I knew that boy was bad news when I went down to Opp to recruit him back in the 70s," Bryant said. "You can take the boy out of the country but you can't take the country out of the boy."

I informed Bryant that DuBose probably would be fired at the end of the season, if not sooner.

"Well, I guess I really can't fault them. Well, who they going to hire?

"Coach, the most prominent names making the rounds are Butch Davis and Frank Beamer."

"You've got to be kidding! They don't have any connection to Alabama. What's happened to this school?"

I didn't really have the heart to tell him. Finally, just to make him feel a little better, I asked Bryant for some suggestions.

"Well, let me think for a minute. What about Danny Ford?"

"Well, Coach, he is out of coaching."

"What about old Charley Pell? He was a good'un."

"The NCAA pretty much ran him out."

"Well, darn, Pat Dye would make a heckuva coach. What about him?"

"Hmm. Don't think it would fly."

"OK, then what's wrong with Jackie Sherrill? He was a cocky son of a gun. But a fine coach."

"Coach, his reputation makes Alabama people a little nervous."

There was a long period of silence. I strained to hear what he was saying. Finally, kneeling down, closing my eyes and concentrating, I heard a faint sound. Then, it became louder.

Bryant was crying.

"Coach, are you OK?"

"I'm sorry," Bryant said. "I get a little emotional thinking about what's happened to my old school."

I tried to cheer him up. I said brighter days were on the horizon. Then I bid adieu.

As I walked away toward the car, I heard him speaking. I stopped and listened, edging closer to the marker.

"Cut us a little slack if you can," Bryant said, plaintively.

No problem, I told the Bear.

"What a mess," Bryant said, in a hushed tone. "I can't believe what has happened. If we keep this up at Alabama, we're going to be a bigger laughingstock than that silly old Cow College down the road."

GOLF IS GOING WAY OF SOCIETY

September 29, 1999

Go ahead. Wave the American flag. Stand tall and sing "I'm proud to be an American." Beat your chest and say, "So what if the Europeans didn't like it? They do the same thing across the pond."

And you wonder why this country is going down the toilet.

What happened Sunday at the Ryder Cup was an outrage.

No, I'm not talking about the reaction of the American team and wives when they ran out and congratulated Justin Leonard after the 45-foot putt to return the Ryder Cup to America. While unfortunate, it's difficult to control emotions at a time like that.

What embarrassed me was the gauche behavior of the crowd at The Country Club of Brookline. What was appalling was the jeering of the European players, the way they were taunted and mocked and insulted by the largely American crowd. It was so bad that Colin Montgomerie's 70-year-old father (fresh off heart surgery) had to leave the course because of the stress.

What a disgrace.

And it's only going to get worse.

The sport of golf, the last bastion of sportsmanship in the world, has now been driven down to the level of a snake's belly. You can find better behavior in the fraternity section at Bryant-Denny Stadium or in the infield at Talladega Superspeedway. Anywhere, probably, but the Ole Miss section at a game involving Tommy Tuberville.

This isn't to say the golfers aren't spoiled and a bunch of prima donnas. So what? What's the point of booing and hissing and jeering? The one thing that has always impressed me about the Europeans is their appreciation of the game. They don't cheer wildly when someone hits a bad shot or even an average shot. But they do applaud when the shot commands regard.

They are proud of their native sons but still can recognize the talents of others, whether they are from Tanzania or Tennessee.

But this is the new culture of sports where everyone is trying to play: "Can you top this?"

Perhaps I really shouldn't be surprised. When you consider the popularity of Jerry Springer and the World Wrestling Federation, perhaps this is golf's next frontier.

What's next? Fist fights at the 18th hole with Springer trying to break up the melee in order to get the round in before dark?

Golf is not for everyone. It has the reputation of being an old man's sport, although one would have a hard time convincing Nike, considering the tons of money being tossed at Tiger Woods.

Still, I asked a fellow not long ago if he played golf. He was in his late 50s.

"Nope, I don't play," he said. "I don't know anyone who plays golf who still enjoys a regular sex life."

Of course, while on the subject, it looked like everyone in the crowd Sunday at Brookline had been shot up with testosterone on the way through the front gates.

Honestly, the scene wasn't much different six weeks ago at Medinah during the final round of the PGA Championship. Only there, most of the Americans were cheering for Sergio Garcia, the 19-year-old Spaniard who was trying to catch Tiger Woods.

Golf is a sport based on integrity. It is the only one where competitors call penalties on themselves, sometimes at the risk of disqualification.

Meanwhile, you turn on an NFL game or college football game and players are doing everything and anything in an attempt to fool the officials, in a desperate effort to win.

There are no solutions, partly, because as golf expands in

popularity, legions of new fans join in the fun and frivolity. That doesn't make it wrong. The sport was too stuffy in the past and mainly was for the elite.

Fortunately, those old crusty doors have been broken down. But education is necessary.

The American conquest Sunday was something special. It truly was one of the greatest sporting moments of the century. Unfortunately, the boorish behavior of the fans (and, to a small part, the American competitors) took some of the shine off the glorious victory.

DREAMS DO COME TRUE

October 4, 1999

GAINESVILLE, Fla. – This wasn't a football game. This was like a trip to Fantasy Island.

Two days later, I'm still not sure what happened Saturday at The Swamp. Did Alabama really defeat the Florida Gators in their own house?

I know Orlando, FL., is down the turnpike from Gainesville, FL., but don't tell me Walt Disney didn't come up with this script. It was too Goofy, too Mickey Mouse to make any sense. This was "Field of Dreams," "Rocky" and "Rudy" wrapped into one.

At the rate Alabama Coach Mike DuBose is going, he'll be firing University of Alabama President Andrew Sorensen shortly instead of the other way around.

Regardless of your feelings toward DuBose, you really have to hand it to Alabama's embattled coach.

Somehow, some way, against the most incredible odds and suffocating pressure I have ever seen a coach face, DuBose has led Alabama back from oblivion.

Finebaum Said...

Some people will say dumb luck prevailed when common sense was thrown out of the Swamp. It would be easy to look for negatives with this man, considering what has happened in the past. It would be easy to snicker (and some people already have) at the fact that in his postgame comments, he gave credit to God.

However, until someone comes up with a better explanation of what happened, I'll defer to DuBose on this one.

Ever heard the phrase: Not in a million years? Well, it will be a million years before a game has a more bizarre and inexplicable finish.

Still, in a year of bombshells, shockers, exposes and screaming National Enquirer headlines, nothing could stop the startling scene Saturday afternoon.

It was illusory. It was frenzied. And it was scrumptious, if you wear crimson.

Florida coach Steve Spurrier might never get over it. But perhaps the biggest question of the day -other than who do you call to start reserving SEC championship game tickets- is what does it mean for DuBose's future?

A fortnight ago, the man's coaching career was dead. Now, hardly anyone knows what to make out of the turnaround.

One can only imagine what Sorensen must have been thinking about Saturday. His current school defeated his old school and he should have been the happiest man in America.

Something tells me he needed an emotional rescue at the end of the day.

The man is in a pickle. Some people now will try to push him into a public show of support for DuBose. One renowned news media man already has led the parade only he started before the Florida game.

Danny Sheridan, the sports analyst for *USA Today*, said last week on Birmingham television that "at the minimum, Coach DuBose should be allowed to finish the season and coach next year without interference."

On Sunday, Sheridan -who has been the only person in the news media to endorse DuBose publicly during the recent turmoil- said the people in charge at Alabama should give him a public show of support immediately.

"They should have done this when they made the decision to retain him (in August)," Sheridan said. "To not do this now sends a very confusing signal to recruits and the present coaching staff, plus -I can assure you- it makes Alabama's rivals very happy."

Until now, this story primarily has been a local and regional story. The national media has paid scant attention. Now that has changed.

Should Alabama continue to win -and DuBose somehow manage to keep his job- the football factory label will be cemented on the side of Denny Chimes. Sorensen will be stamped as the academician who sold out principles for bowl trips. Firing DuBose is a dangerous route, too.

Right now, perhaps the best course for Sorensen is to maintain a stiff upper lip and keep a keg-sized bottle of Advil nearby.

Two weeks ago, even the most zealous Alabama fan wasn't convinced the Tide would win again during the 1999 season. Now, one has to wonder if the Tide will lose again.

Imagine Bobby Bowden vs. DuBose in the Sugar Bowl for the national championship. That's not any stranger than the thought of what happened Saturday. (Of course, to get to The Big Easy, DuBose probably will have to scalp Spurrier again at the Georgia Dome.)

In defeating Florida, Alabama has overcome the biggest obstacle on its regular-season schedule. Despite what has happened off the field, this team has come together in splendid fashion.

One could sense the overwhelming desire to win for the entire 60 minutes (and change) against Florida. You have to give DuBose and his staff a tip of the hat. The game balls (other than the automatic one each week to Shaun Alexander) must go to defensive coordinator Ellis Johnson, whose group kept Alabama in the game, and Charlie Stubbs, the real star of this show. Alabama's quarterback coach called the game of his life.

Two weeks ago, rumors were swirling that Stubbs was finished in the wake of DuBose disregarding his game plan against Louisiana Tech. The other day, Stubbs sounded like a beaten man. Now, he probably will be getting offers from all over the nation.

So what happens now?

I don't really know. And I doubt you do, either.

I am sure of one thing: This already has been one of the most incomprehensible football seasons anyone has seen. And it's not even half over.

Just when you thought nothing could top the August rumors and revelations about DuBose and his secretary, coupled with the shocker against Louisiana Tech and upset over Arkansas, the Tide goes to the toughest arena in college football and pulls out the most extraordinary victory in modern time over the game's best coach.

I will close with the following caveat: This will be my last column for a while. By the time you read this, I will be in Hollywood writing the screenplay to "The Mike DuBose Story."

HERE'S THE FIRST VOTE FOR TIDE'S ALEXANDER

October 9, 1999

So how am I going to vote in the upcoming election?

It's a question being asked around the state of Alabama today. It is an important decision and I have considered the issues very closely and carefully. And ladies and gentleman, when it comes time to fill out my ballot, I will vote with both conscious and conviction. The fat-cat lobbyists won't impact my decision. Neither will any of the special interest groups nor slick commercials or placards or scare tactics.

When the time comes, I simply will close my eyes, take a deep breath and write in the name of Shaun Alexander on my ballot for Heisman Trophy.

Two weeks ago, and I'm in a confessional mode now, I scoffed at the thought. I thought Alexander's run for the Heisman was toast. I thought Warren Beatty had a better chance of being elected president than Alexander had of winning the Heisman.

After all, Alabama was losing. The program was in turmoil and the Tide seemed headed for a season on the brink instead of the SEC Championship game.

But a combination of events have turned in Alexander's favor. Certainly, Alexander's display against Arkansas and Florida were breathtaking and unforgettable. And he's been consistently good each week.

When I heard about the arrest of Heisman favorite Peter Warrick, the Florida State star receiver whose speed can burn defensive backs in a nanosecond but who isn't fast enough to outrun the law, my mind began to wander.

The Heisman is an individual award. However, there is more to the story. After his arrest, Warrick didn't show any penitence.

Instead, he responded to questions, saying: "Hey, I didn't kill the president."

No, but he might have killed his Heisman chances.

I don't care if he comes back from the doghouse or the jail house or whatever and catches five touchdown passes per quarter and leads the Seminoles to a national title. This clown is off my short list.

On the other hand, you had Alexander a week ago on national television, after the biggest victory of his life, and did he high-five for the cameras? Did he gloat that his team has proved the experts wrong? Did he trash talk like some of the thugs roaming the college gridirons?

None of the above.

Alexander talked about his faith and his beliefs. He complimented his embattled head coach.

Alexander stands tall in front of millions of young Americans about what's right in the world.

Now, don't misunderstand the point here. I think the people who vote should consider the total worth to a football team in assessing someone's ability, from talent on the field to leadership in the locker room.

I'm not sure in all of my years of covering football if I have seen one individual worth more to a club in both departments than Alexander has been worth this year to Alabama.

I won't waste your time with a laundry list of his stats. I mean, the Florida defensive coaches thought they had done a good job of containing Alexander in the Swamp. What did he do? Alexander broke their hearts (and backs) twice when the game was on the line.

You take Alexander away from this team and Alabama still has talent, but probably not the unity necessary to give the Tide a shot at the title.

And to think he didn't have to stay in school. With a degree under his belt, Alexander could have gone off to the NFL and been cashing a big check every Sunday. However, like Peyton Manning did in a similar situation two years ago in Knoxville, Alexander wanted more time in Tuscaloosa and perhaps a legitimate run at the Heisman.

Right now, Alexander is in a strong position to win the coveted award. A number of Internet sites have shown him at or near the top spot.

Things can change.

Unfortunately, one bad day for Alexander and the Tide can knock him back to the pack or out of the race. The key to the whole thing might be whether Warrick comes back. He might be the single most talented player in the nation. But is he the most valuable?

In the past, I have had mixed emotions about the importance of the Heisman Trophy. I think the news media puts too much pressure on the award, turning the race into sport's version of the Iowa Caucus and New Hampshire presidential primary.

The analysis is done with little thought and a lot of bluster. Perhaps I also am getting caught up in the moment here with my declaration for Alexander. Some people might say if I lived in Birmingham, Mich., instead of Birmingham, Ala., I wouldn't be saying this.

However, every once in a while, a special athlete comes along and changes the thought process. Two years ago, Manning was one of those remarkable athletes, and writers from the Midwest and the East robbed him by giving the award to a defensive wizard from the Wolverines.

Considering what has gone wrong recently with Alabama football, it would be nice to see the school finally get a Heisman Trophy winner. And what better person to end Alabama's drought in that department than to see Shaun Alexander holding the trophy in early December?

IS THIS GAME A DRESS REHEARSAL?

November 13, 1999

At the age of 55 and entering the autumn of his career, Jackie Sherrill returns today to his alma mater with perhaps his last and best chance at making a favorable impression on the people who routinely have spurned his efforts to become the Alabama head coach.

It would be premature to say Mike DuBose's coaching career hangs in the balance today. It would be equally absurd to say this decisive game for the Southeastern Conference Western Division championship won't factor into his future, that is, assuming his tenure at Alabama hasn't already been settled in a smoke-filled room.

And here comes Sherrill, the wily veteran who nearly scaled college football's summit at Pittsburgh and Texas A&M and then fell completely off the charts, only to climb back up the hill, that is, as high as one can go at a school such as Mississippi State - the K-Mart of college football programs.

Sherrill says he is happy at State. But longtime Sherrill watchers believe the MSU coach would crawl to Tuscaloosa if given the opportunity to take over the one job he has always coveted.

Perhaps the larger question is whether Alabama would dare to hire him. Certainly, Sherrill has the lineage. He played for Paul Bryant and served for a year as a graduate assistant at the paw of the "Bear."

A victory today would mark four consecutive victories over his alma mater. Sherrill owns three consecutive victories over Auburn. So that vexing Bill Curry question goes right off the board.

Interestingly, it was Sherrill's first victory over Alabama in 1996 (by virtue of a missed extra point when the Tide was a 12-

point favorite in Starkville, Miss.) that might have saved his job. At the time, the State program was floundering and fans had just about had their fill of Sherrill's drivel. In 1993, the Bulldogs had been tied by Arkansas State. In 1995, in the midst of a 3-8 season, they had lost to Northeast Louisiana.

Now the Bulldogs, coming off an SEC West title in 1998, are undefeated through eight games this season. It's the best start in MSU history.

The Tide has turned.

In some respects, Sherrill would be a nice fit at Alabama. He knows how to recruit in the SEC. He has been successful at Pittsburgh, Texas A&M and now MSU.

However, would Alabama hire a man -some four years after their own school was hit with major NCAA sanctions- who has one of the worst reputations in college coaching? Some people have referred to Sherrill as the Darth Vader of coaching. Other people have not been so nice.

In fairness to Sherrill, the Bulldogs have had only one minor brush with the NCAA since his arrival in 1991. However, you can bet the NCAA's file on Sherrill is thicker than the New York City phone book.

The trepidation in hiring Sherrill is the same as getting close to a skunk. If you get too close, you're bound to get sprayed by something unsavory.

Many years ago, someone once asked Joe Paterno if he would ever consider leaving college for the NFL.

Jo Pa said absolutely not, adding, "I don't want to leave the game to the Jackie Sherrills and Barry Switzers of the world."

When it comes to being a cold fish, Sherrill retired the trophy.

Last spring, I sat with him doing a radio show. He was promoting a book about the greatest moments in MSU history. Not surprisingly, it was a very thin book.

The subject turned to golf. I mentioned a recent game with Tommy Tuberville, with whom he has had a frosty relationship over the years. I said Tub had belted some of his drives over 300 yards.

"When I played a lot of golf, I could knock it farther than that," Sherrill said. "Nobody could outdrive me."

I started to ask him how many green jackets he had won at Augusta but decided against it.

The coach has had brushes with almost everyone in the game. He got flack over castrating a bull before a game against Texas. He accused Auburn of putting helium in the balls.

But the criticism rolls off Sherrill. It's always the other person's fault.

I spent nearly an entire weekend with Sherrill in 1988 in College Station, Texas, when Curry cancelled Alabama's game at Texas A&M because of a hurricane that never came. That Friday night, I had dinner with Sherrill and his wife at the time. I believe it was wife No. 2, but with Sherrill, keeping up with his number of wives can be a full-time job. I believe he is currently on No. 3, but who's counting?

We had breakfast the next day and spent four hours in a sports bar watching football (he didn't have a game and my flight wasn't until the next day). I don't think he said a memorable thing the entire day. Well, that is, other than how he could be running the Alabama athletic department considerably better than it was being run at the time and coaching better than Curry.

He probably was right on both accounts.

If for whatever reason DuBose is let go, Sherrill would be an interesting replacement.

But would Alabama people feel comfortable with Sherrill at the helm? Would anyone other than a desperate, backwoods school such as Mississippi State feel good with this man in charge?

These are tough questions, but these also are difficult times. Sherrill has come many miles over the years in an effort to rehabilitate one of the most unsavory reputations in college football history.

With each move over his career, Sherrill has inched closer to Alabama, the one job he has always coveted.

However, in the end, those final 87 miles of dusty roads from Starkville to Tuscaloosa probably will prove too much for Jackie Sherrill to overcome.

DUBOSE'S CAREER MIGHT BE ON LINE

November 20, 1999

By now, we have all heard the joke. It has been making the rounds in Alabama since the first leaves began falling off trees in mid-October.

This week, the nice woman who does the pest control at our house rushed inside from the whipping wind and breathlessly said:

"Have you heard what the board of trustees is going to do with Mike DuBose if Alabama beats Auburn?"

I shook my head and shrugged (after all, she had rat poisoning in her hand).

"They are going to let him start dating again."

Pretty funny, huh?

Unfortunately, the situation created last August by University of Alabama President Andrew Sorensen and the Board of Trustees is not.

Using common sense and common decency, DuBose should have been fired. The man disgraced the position of head football coach at the University of Alabama. He brought shame to the school and its storied football legacy.

By lying about his relationship with a university employee,

he put the institution in a precarious legal predicament and helped create a rupture between the school's president and Board of Trustees some doubt can ever be repaired.

At first, we wondered if DuBose would make it to the end of the week. Remember when everyone had a friend who heard the story about. ... Then, after the loss to Louisiana Tech, we wondered if he would be fired after the Arkansas or Florida games.

The cowardice of Sorensen to do the right thing in August coupled with a group of social butterflies on the board of trustees -who look better suited to be in charge of picking the pin positions for the country club golf championship than running a university system- created a circus atmosphere.

Amazingly, this football team pulled together, whether it was the coaching of DuBose or Charlie Stubbs threatening to quit or dumb luck or all of the above, combined with having the nation's best offensive lineman and one of the top running backs.

Here we are now, at that familiar 11th game on the schedule, and Alabama is two victories away from a Bowl Championship Series berth and an outside shot at the national title.

And guess what? The president and board of trustees are getting what they deserve: egg spread evenly all over their faces. Things have changed so dramatically that trustee Joe Fine, who led the move to fire DuBose in August, reversed fields this week and endorsed the Alabama head coach. Fine said DuBose should be retained even if the Tide loses to Auburn.

Pardon me while I gag over Fine's sincerity.

Does anyone really believe this man? This would be like former independent prosecutor Ken Starr, who tried to run Bill Clinton out of office, suddenly changing directions and saying he and Slick Willy are buds for life.

Although most insiders believe Fine's flip flop was cheesy and disingenuous, give the man credit. He's no dummy. Fine is a cunning politician, and you don't need to be a weatherman to see which way the wind is blowing in this state.

Finebaum Said...

With a victory tonight, DuBose will have traveled from the state's biggest joke to a potential finalist for the Paul "Bear" Bryant Award, given to the national coach of the year.

Is Sorensen going to fire a coach who goes 9-2 and defeats Auburn at Jordan-Hare Stadium? On what grounds?

If he tried it, the only one being fired would be the school president. Of course, there is rampant speculation DuBose could be a goner if he loses tonight.

Tim Brando, the CBS college football host, said this week he had been told by reliable sources (whatever that means):

"DuBose is gone if he loses to Auburn. It's as simple as that."

I asked Sid McDonald, the president pro tem of the board of trustees, this week if he is personally in favor of DuBose returning next year. The man hemmed and hawed and finally blew so much hot air in my direction, I thought I was caught in the middle of a West Texas dust storm. (I just wish Regis Philbin had been around to ask McDonald if that was his final answer.)

As for tonight, it goes without saying that beating Auburn is important.

Members of the university's board have backed themselves into such a corner that a victory might not only force the school to retain DuBose but give him back the two years on his contract taken away in August.

What kind of message would that send?

It's OK to lie and cheat and deceive, as long as you say you're sorry, and most important, as long as you just win, baby.

Clinton remained president because we have a good economy. The public gave him a pass because they were happy with their own lives. Why rock the boat when the sun is out and the winds are calm and the trains are running on time?

The same story has happened here with DuBose. Alabama football fans care about what's right and wrong. They are good and decent people who work hard during the week. But remember, these are football fans, who enjoy nothing more than seeing their beloved team win on Saturday.

They might feel differently if the scandal touched their pastor or local school superintendent. However, a winning season and beating Auburn can go a long way toward soothing other ailments.

So the stage is set tonight.

Will it be DuBose's last stand? Or will an historic victory over Auburn put an end to his uncertain status and launch his career at Alabama into orbit?

It often has been said that the Iron Bowl is about the players, about what happens on the field. However, this year, the biggest story might be going on off the field.

A coaching career hangs in the balance. And to some people, so does the good name and reputation of a university.

FOR MOORE, SCHOOL TIES, LOYALTY FINALLY PAY OFF

November 24, 1999

It was a cold and rainy December day and journalists were everywhere. Paul William Bryant had just officially announced his retirement and Ray Perkins had been tabbed as his replacement.

The year was 1982.

As reporters made mad dashes for the phones and camera crews began to pack up, I made my way down the long hallway of the football offices.

Secretaries were wailing. Some coaches were busy on the phone, probably looking for jobs. Other staffers stood around, still dazed by the events.

I caught one office door barely cracked and made a gut call

to knock.

"Come in," said the hushed voice of Mal Moore.

I walked in with my notebook glued to my right hand. I started to talk but couldn't make out a word.

Moore's face was still, almost Mount Rushmore-like. He was so inert, I would have sworn he had just been embalmed.

Finally, I took a deep breath and asked the proverbial "how-do-you-feel?" question. I was still a young buck and really didn't know any better.

Moore's eyes twitched for a moment, signifying rigor mortis had not yet set in. After a long pause, Moore said: "I have no comment. Would you just let me off the hook with that?"

I started to bear in and ask a follow up. After all, Moore, who was offensive coordinator for Bryant during his final years, had been considered a front-runner for the job. There had been whispers that Bryant had told him personally he was the top choice.

Of course, Gene Stallings had heard the same whispers. So had others.

Then, Moore dropped his head, looking at me like a hound dog when waking up. I could have dumped a hot pot of coffee on his head and he wasn't going to say anything else. I quietly walked out of the room.

What else could be said? The pain and suffering of the man was excruciating to watch. Not only had Moore lost out on the head job, Perkins was not going to retain him as play-caller. And he knew it.

So it was off to Notre Dame to work for Gerry Faust, and then to the NFL before Moore was back in Tuscaloosa. His tenure under Stallings at Alabama -although successful on the field- was not particularly satisfying.

His wife became seriously ill. Meanwhile, Tide fans, dejected with the predictable offense, were calling for Moore's head during a disappointing 1993 season, which saw the Tide's record fall to 9-3-1 after 11-1 and 13-0 seasons.

Moore was kicked upstairs to shuffle papers. His name surfaced for the vacant athletic director's job in 1996, but there was a push to go outside the program.

Bob Bockrath took Moore around to alumni groups before putting him in charge of courtesy cars used by athletic department officials. What an important responsibility!

Interestingly, Moore never whined. He was a loyal soldier, and perhaps that is why he was given the job of athletic director Tuesday.

Clearly, he doesn't meet the criterion given by University of Alabama President Andrew Sorensen. Of course, this has become more the norm than the exception under Sorensen's administration when it comes to hiring athletic department officials.

Will Moore make a good athletic director?

Probably.

People like Moore. Clearly, he understands as well as anyone the tradition of the school and the day-to-day operations of the athletic department.

"He was the most impressive person we interviewed in 1996," said one person, who was on the search committee. "He blew us away with his answers."

There were similar comments this time around.

While many supporters of Mike DuBose have viewed Moore's hiring as a major break, others aren't so sure. While DuBose lives to see another day as Alabama's head football coach, he now will be judged by someone who once coached in a milieu where a 9-2 season was considered a fiasco.

Tuesday, Moore painstakingly praised DuBose without making a definitive statement on his future.

Watching Moore this season in the press box take notes during games has been interesting. I have seen him wince at times after a questionable call by DuBose.

Some people might regard Moore's hiring as a step backward for the school. Perhaps a younger person, one whose skills were in marketing and public relations, would have been better. Of course, fitting in at Alabama always has been more important than any other trait.

Using that as a measuring stick, Alabama has found the right man in Moore.

The former quarterback and assistant coach never got the job he always coveted. He never got to run the football program.

However, after years of remaining on the sidelines, in the background, Moore finally has seen the sunlight, as he is now the man to lead the Alabama athletic department into the next millennium.

BOWDEN DOESN'T COMPARE TO 'BEAR'

January 8, 2000

A second national championship is behind him and an assault on a legendary record is ahead of him, so the comparisons will be made early and often in the next few years.

The comparisons, that is, between Bobby Bowden and Paul "Bear" Bryant.

There are many similarities and many distinct differences. But the most striking, the most glaring -other than the winning- comes from the brood.

Bryant's son, Paul Jr., never has been heard to speak above a whisper, and few people have heard him talk at all.

Bowden's son Terry hasn't stopped since the baby doctor slapped him at delivery.

The old joke used to go: "Once, Terry's wife didn't talk to him for three weeks. She didn't want to interrupt him."

Bryant's son always seems to be sulking over something important. Meanwhile, someone once cracked that Terry looks like a Boy Scout who just made Eagle.

Well, I think you get the idea about the SOBBs: the Sons of Bowden and Bryant.

Let's start with the record. Although Grambling's Eddie Robinson smashed Bryant's record of 323 career victories years ago and Joe Paterno is likely to reach the target next season, most people believe Bowden will own it for good. Currently, he is at 304 victories. He is 70 years old, and apparently only one scenario will keep him from breaking the coveted record.

Some critics will claim Bowden's record is a paper tiger. One must agree.

Paterno has spent his entire career at Penn State and Bryant earned his victories the old-fashioned way at Maryland, Kentucky, Texas A&M and Alabama, but Bowden fattened his record with victories at Howard (now Samford) before heading to West Virginia and FSU.

Of Bowden's victories, 31 were compiled at the Birmingham school. The schedule at Howard will severely test the needle on the Giggle Meter.

Have a yen for marshmallows and creampuffs?

How about victories over the likes of Gordon Military College, Maryville, Tennessee Tech's B-team, Georgetown (of Kentucky), Delta State, Memphis Navy (a 40-0 job), Southwestern of Memphis (wonder how Bobby missed out on Elvis' touch football team while he was scouring Memphis for games), National University of Mexico (60-0) and an epic battle against Troy State (an 80-0 victory in 1961 that included 12 touchdowns - eight rushing, three passing and one punt return)?

Unfortunately, you're remembered by how you leave, and Bowden's last game at Howard was a bitter loss to McNeese State in the Civitan Bowl (no, I don't think that was a BCS game).

Bryant wasn't afraid to take on anyone in his hey-day,

evidenced by regular-season games against Nebraska, Notre Dame, Southern Cal, Washington and Penn State. One nonconference opponent, the 1966 opener against Louisiana Tech, probably cost him a third consecutive national title.

Bowden built his name in the late '70s and early 80's by not only playing the big schools, but playing them on the road.

At the time, Bowden begged to get into the Southeastern Conference, but he was shunned. However, when the tables were reversed a decade ago, Bowden said thanks but no thanks. FSU joined the pathetically easy Atlantic Coast Conference, and frankly, I think most legitimate fans forever will hold this against the coach in terms of objectively comparing his record to Bryant's.

In Bowden's favor, FSU played Miami and Florida every year. But it didn't mean quite as much, considering the Seminoles also were playing Duke, North Carolina State, Maryland and the other powder-puff girls' teams from the nation's best basketball conference.

The most striking statistic about Bowden concerns 13 consecutive top-four finishes in the AP poll.

Bryant never came close to such an achievement. Of course, the Bear was playing a more competitive regular-season schedule. Bryant compiled nine consecutive top 10 finishes between 1959-1967.

Bryant also was winning during this time while segregation was in full bloom. Alabama won five national championships in the AP Poll under Bryant and four in the UPI coaches' poll. UPI awarded Alabama the 1973 championship before the bowl game (which the Crimson Tide lost to Notre Dame). That was laughable. However, nobody was laughing when UPI awarded the national title to USC in 1978 after Alabama defeated Penn State in the Sugar Bowl (in the so-called national title game). Of course, the Tide had lost to USC earlier in the season at Legion Field.

On the other hand, Alabama should have won at least two more titles under Bryant, in 1966 when the Tide was undefeated (the title went to Notre Dame, which had played for a tie against Michigan State) and in 1977, when the Irish leapfrogged from No. 5 to No. 1 after defeating top-ranked Texas.

Bowden's first title in 1993 was absurd, considering he beat out Notre Dame, which had beaten his team on the field. This year's title certainly was legitimate, although many people believe Nebraska was a better team.

Of course, in fairness to Bowden, there have been several years when his team probably was the nation's best team but finished second. FSU fans believe the Seminoles could have whipped Alabama in 1992, which is silly, considering Florida State lost to Miami, the team Alabama crushed 34-13 in the Sugar Bowl.

In 1996, FSU whipped Florida and then had to turn around and play the Gators. The rematch in the Sugar Bowl was a Gator blowout.

Bryant's career also spanned generations of great change, from the war babies through the baby boomers and the dawning of black players, to the "me generation" of the 80s.

Bowden also has spanned a long period and he has adjusted well. However, with the changing times, Bowden has craned his neck even more. He has looked the other way in terms of discipline, which is a black mark on his career. Also, he has benefited from the state of Florida emerging as a recruiting hotbed.

Another glaring difference between the two men was displayed Tuesday night, when Bowden granted a live interview on ABC during the second quarter of the game.

Had Lynn Swann tried to interview Bryant during a game- heck for that matter, during a spring scrimmage- the sportscaster would have ended up eating dirt.

Of all the differences between the two men, the most glaring contrast is in the aforementioned area of discipline.

Bryant's discipline was legendary, from suspending Joe Namath on down. Bowden's record on discipline is pitiful. You almost have to be accused of first-degree murder to get tossed off a Bobby Bowden team.

Even today, pick a Bryant disciple, from any generation, and they will get choked up talking about the Bear. Case in point: Namath's interview during the Orange Bowl telecast.

About the only former FSU player who gets sniffles talking about Bowden is Burt Reynolds. The actor (well, that is a debatable description) didn't even play for Bowden. Besides, it's hard to find many of Bowden's former players, unless, you make a quick visit to the Florida state penitentiary.

For that reason, above all else, Bryant's legacy will far outlast that of Bowden in the annals of football history. Both are great coaches. Both have the records to prove the point.

However, Bryant never sold out principles for victories. In this category, Bowden couldn't carry the Bear's jock strap.

HE WAS TRULY A WONDERFUL YOUNG MAN

February 9, 2000

I was unpacking a new computer when the phone rang Tuesday morning. It was the newspaper, and they had heard a report that Derrick Thomas had died.

"I don't think so," I replied, continuing to unpack a box as I talked.

"That's what we heard," the fellow continued.

"Well, that can't be true," I countered. "One of his closest friends called me yesterday (Monday) about setting up an interview with him in Miami. Derrick was feeling better and wanted to let everyone back here know how he was doing."

I hung up quickly, calling my friend and as he answered the

phone, the sound of hurt and shock told me all I needed to know.

"It's true about Derrick, isn't it?" I said.

"Yep. It happened a few minutes ago."

I hung up the phone slowly and stared into space.

By the time I could catch my breath, ESPN was interrupting a story on Tiger Woods to make it official. Then it was back to regular programming.

So what can you say at a time like this? What can anyone say or do to make the hurt go away? How can you put in words the effects of the tragedy of this fine young man?

What was so stunning was that the report on Thomas a day earlier had been so upbeat. So many friends had come by and called. Dennis Erickson had just been by for a visit. Jerry Rice had called and catered a Super Bowl party in his room a week ago. Howard Cross was there at the time. Other outings were being planned.

Sure, Thomas faced the biggest challenge of his life, to learn to maneuver a wheelchair and face the darkness that often would lurk behind the unmarked doors. Still, he seemed sanguine, and while doctors gave him a slim chance of ever walking, the former Alabama superstar seemed to be taking the challenge in stride.

Suddenly, Tuesday, it was over.

Some people might say his young body simply couldn't handle the trauma of what had transpired in the past two weeks, of seeing his closest friend die in his car and of having his legs taken away from him, his career ending.

Who really knows why Thomas' heart quit beating? Who really knows the answer to any of these questions, other than what a doctor says?

What should never be forgotten was the life he left behind, the contributions he made, the impact he had on his family, his friends and his teammates, to say nothing of fans all over the nation.

We all tend to push the hyperbole meter at times like this.

Finebaum Said...

We tend to stretch the truth when talking about someone who has died, to make more out his life in death than what is really merited.

With Derrick Thomas, one doesn't have to push the button very hard, because he truly was a wonderful young man.

Everyone has his or her own special memory of something Derrick did on the field or off. But from here, it was his smile, his charm, his personality off the field that always meant more to me than the All-America trophies or the nine All-Pro honors in his spectacular NFL career.

During his college career and during those many times afterward, when he would come back to an Alabama game or call about an occasional golf match while passing through town, he was always kind, oozing with personality and charisma.

That was Derrick Thomas, and now he is gone.

What a loss, but also what a lesson to others. In an age when NFL players are filling up the police blotter and county jails, Thomas was different.

He enjoyed life to the fullest. But you didn't have to worry about bailing him out of jail. Now, because of a tragic accident- and because he failed to buckle his seat belt- he is gone.

There won't be that interview scheduled for later this week. There won't be the process of watching Thomas overcome yet another challenge in his life, and seeing him stand tall as a beacon of light for others.

But his life will live on in our memory. It is a life worth remembering, honoring and cherishing.

COWBOYS' IMAGE CAME FROM COACH

February 14, 1994

I would love to be able to engage you today with Tom Landry stories, like so many of my Texas colleagues.

That's the thing to do when a legend dies. We search back through old yarns and hit reboot on our memory banks, and the anecdotes flow like smooth Tennessee whiskey on a cool, Saturday night.

I might have talked to the man three times in my life, once when Gene Stallings was being interviewed for the Birmingham Stallions head coaching position. Another time when Stallings was hired at Alabama. The final time, a few years ago, when Landry was pushing his autobiography.

The first was one of the scariest interviews in my career. I called the Cowboys' headquarters and asked if I could speak with the man referred to as Old Stone Face. His secretary called me back and said he would call me back at 9:15 a.m. the next day. At 9:15 a.m. the next day -not 9:14 or 9:16- the phone rang and it was a stoic man from the television pictures, dressed in the dark business suit, the hat and the eternal frown. He couldn't have been nicer.

It was one of the rare moments in journalism when the cynicism evaporates and one is genuinely impressed with something that has happened or is happening.

When I was young, the Cowboys were my team. Don't ask me why, other than they were everyone else's as well. They were America's Team, so they might as well have been mine.

I loved Roger Staubach and Tony Dorsett and everything associated with the Cowboys. Of course, it was hard not to like the Cowboys in the 1970s as they raced toward five Super Bowl appearances.

While I cheered the Cowboys, I merely tolerated Landry. Later in life, after I began to read and understand, but particularly after hearing Landry stories from Stallings, I really began to appreciate the genius of this simple but multifaceted individual.

Unfortunately, we often are remembered for our exits from the public arena, and few people, if any, have left the stage in a worse light than Landry. The man who took the Cowboys to the pinnacle left football after a pathetic 3-13 season and a public execution by new owner Jerry Jones.

In the years after Landry was fired, my love for the Cowboys died a cruel death. Perhaps if I had known more about what was really going on in Dallas under his reign, I would have bailed out earlier.

Landry probably was not everything he appeared to be during those glory days. Probably not even close.

While Landry looked the other way, a modern-day Rome was falling all around him. Of course, he knew what was going on. He chose to ignore the den of iniquity.

Perhaps columnist Skip Bayless, who often skewered Landry for being too old and out of touch, put it best in a book entitled, "God's Coach: The Hymns, Hype, and Hypocrisy of Tom Landry's Cowboys." Bayless compared Landry to the Wizard of Oz, relating the story of Dorothy, in tears and enraged, telling the wizard: "Oh, you're a very bad man."

The wizard answered: "Oh, no, my dear. I'm a very good man. I'm just a very bad wizard."

Landry was a rare breed. While he won't be remembered in the same breath as Vince Lombardi or Bear Bryant, arguably the best NFL coach and the best college coach of the past 50 years, Landry wasn't far behind.

However, in terms of role models -a word that seemingly is verboten now when speaking of the NFL- Landry was the best. At a time when people were forbidden to wear religion on their sleeve, Landry stood tall and told anyone who would listen.

Wherever he went during his life, Thomas Wade Landry commanded respect.

That respect probably will follow him in death.

SIR CHARLES, TONIGHT MAY BE FINALE BUT STAY IN TOUCH

April 19, 2000

Why should anyone really be surprised? Why should our eyebrows raise and our tongues wag one more time, now that Sir Chuck has come up with yet another way of elongating his NBA career?

When it comes to our Charles Barkley, why ask why?

Tonight, in Houston, Barkley waves goodbye for the last time. We think.

When we last saw Barkley on the basketball court in Philadelphia, he was being carted off in wrenching pain. The moment his aging body came down on the hardwood, everyone knew it was over. It was, the good doctors said, a career-ending injury.

Barkley took a television job for TNT and has been working on his abject golf game. He made noise about coming back. However, this was a guy who couldn't get in shape when he was young. How in the world was he going to manage now, at the age of 37 and in fading physical condition?

Well, there he was Tuesday night in Phoenix, where he came the closest to that elusive ring (won MVP for the Suns in 1993 and went to the NBA finals). Tonight, he is back in Houston, as the Rockets' season comes to a merciless end.

Finebaum Said...

On a personal note, I have put off writing a valediction to Barkley's career, because how do we really know it is over? After all, Barkley has retired four different times. After all, this is the same fellow who claims he was misquoted in his own autobiography. Now, come on.

Of course, that's why I love the guy, and so does everyone else.

For a man who has gotten into more scrapes than anyone in NBA history -from spitting on the little girl to throwing people out of windows- he has the biggest heart in sports.

The scores of people Barkley has personally given money to, people he didn't even know. ... The millions of money he donated to charities and to his beloved Auburn University. ...The lives he has touched. ...

Oh, there is a ribald side of Sir Charles. He loves to joke with the best of them. He has been known to nurse a drink late into the night. He can trash talk with Michael Jordan on the basketball court and Tiger Woods on the links. However, when his Granny and Mama from Leeds talk to Barkley, there is no talking back. It's "yes, ma'am."

Barkley never has forgotten where he came from and the struggles the aforementioned women had to go through for him and his siblings.

Once, during a golf round, I hit a shot that raced into the woods. I slammed my club down. I had barely slept the night before (believe it or not, I actually was working on a newspaper story) and muttered to no one in particular: "Man, am I having a hard day. This is awful."

Barkley practically grabbed me by the neck and said: "What the ... are you talking about?"

I snapped my head in the air and gave him a basset hound face, turning up in a slightly tilted fashion.

"A hard day is coming home from a factory after making pipes for 12 hours and finding a way to feed your eight kids and pregnant wife," Barkley said. "Man, you've got it made."

Finebaum Said...

He had a point. I didn't complain the rest of the round. I also walked on the other side of the fairway after he hit a bad shot.

Years ago, when I saw him more, I would brag to people about "my friend Charles." Of course, I later found out half the world made the same claim, and with good reason.

Barkley could make a friend while waiting to use a pay phone. Of course, he could get arrested in the same amount of time.

However, I took our friendship so seriously, once I tried to give him advice on the golf course. It nearly ended my life.

Walking with him in 1994 at the Bruno's Memorial Classic, on the infamous day he played with Michael Jordan, I noticed his swing was so fast, it looked as if he was trying to kill a rattlesnake instead of make contact with the golf ball.

With 10,000 people following, his game was beyond the usual embarrassment. I really felt for him. Finally, after he had knocked yet another ball in the water, I awkwardly walked over said: "Charles, you have to slow down. Take a deep breath and bring the club back slowly."

He glared at me, uttered a few choice expletives and stormed away. Well, that was the end of a nice friendship, I mumbled to myself.

Interestingly, at the next hole, Barkley started to yank the club back again. But he stopped. He gulped some air and his swing slowed down. He made contact, and for a couple of holes, he hit the ball nicely. He gave me a quick nod as if to say: Thanks.

I could go on and on with Barkley tales, but I'll leave here on a high note. Tonight's farewell in Houston is the end of his basketball career. But there is so much more for Barkley to do.

No, I don't think he will come back to Alabama and run for governor. I can't imagine Barkley having the patience or the stomach for a job that requires kissing so much derriere.

But I do hope he'll come back and do something in his homeland. He is one of this area's greatest treasures, and we should be able to enjoy his talents more often, even if his basketball days are now over.

MOM WAS ALWAYS A GOOD SPORT

May 13, 2000

Several years ago, in a profile of me in a local magazine, the following passage appeared: "You've got to realize something about Paul Finebaum. He was not as fortunate as some of us were. Paul was abandoned as a child and raised by wolves."

I thought the line was hilarious. All of my friends (both of them) felt the same way. My mother, who found humor in everything, was not amused.

She wanted the man's telephone number and address. She wanted to give him a piece of her mind. Finally, she let it go, much to the benefit of the man's future health.

It is easy on this special spring weekend to wax poetic about mothers. Sunday will mark the sixth Mother's Day without my mom.

Having lost my father at 15, I thought I would be ready and mature enough to handle her passing. I was wrong.

Friends often have encouraged me to write a book about my mother. Others have done so and won Pulitzer Prizes and made millions of dollars and become famous. I once joked that my family wasn't interesting enough for a best-selling book about growing up in the South. Neither my father nor mother was an alcoholic or cheated on each other. They didn't beat me with tire irons. We had indoor plumbing. They came to my Little League baseball games. We went on family trips and sang songs in the car. Pretty tame stuff in today's grunge literary world.

But my mother was a character. I trust those few in the

audience who had the pleasure of meeting her are smiling on that line. Our two favorite subjects -other than my big sister- were politics and sports.

My mother grew up in New York and would revel me with stories about skipping school to go to the old Polo Grounds to watch her beloved Giants play baseball. She was in the hospital about to go into labor with my sister but still had a transistor radio blaring, listening to Bobby Thompson's epic home run in the bottom of the ninth to win the playoff game between the Giants and the Brooklyn Dodgers.

My mother was a disciplinarian of sorts. Yet she let me stay home from school one October day to watch the first game of the World Series between my two favorite teams, the Yankees and the Cardinals. I faked a sore throat, but she knew better.

After my father died, we went to Memphis State basketball games together, once even going to the airport (on a school night) to greet the team after its first victory at Louisville. Afterward, we stopped at IHOP for pecan waffles. I thought my Mom was pretty cool.

We went to the Final Four together when Memphis played UCLA for the NCAA Tournament championship in St. Louis. Gene Bartow was the coach and my mother thought he was the greatest man in town. So did many other people.

After I moved to Birmingham and met people such as Paul Bryant, Joe Namath, Willie Mays, Jack Nicklaus, Bart Starr, Bo Jackson and Charles Barkley, among others, the only one she cared about was Bartow.

Even when Bartow and I weren't on good terms, the UAB coach always made sure my mother had good seats when the Blazers played in Memphis. She once approached Dick Vitale of ESPN, someone I have been friendly with for years, before a game in Memphis. After telling Vitale who she was, she proceeded to give him a piece of her mind about something he had said the week before. Incredibly, she silenced Dickie Vee.

I introduced her to Pat Dye and she told him I hated Bill Curry. I started to interrupt her and tell her to keep quiet.

"Well, it's true, isn't it?" she said as Dye howled.

I took her to an NCAA basketball tournament game in Atlanta between UCLA and UAB. Naturally, she had great seats, right behind the Bartow family. I told her I would come by at half-time from my seat on press row. Naturally, she wanted to come down and visit and I politely told her it was for working media only. I zipped into the media room at halftime to grab a quick drink. There she was, yakking with other writers, picking through the free food and complaining about the poor selection of fruit.

Ten years ago this spring, she came to Birmingham to meet the young doctor I was dating and to whom I was about to become engaged.

The introductions were barely underway, when my mother interrupted my wife to be, saying: "I just want you to know right away that I hate woman doctors."

She proceeded to rattle off all of the past problems she had experienced as I looked for the nearest couch to hide under. My mother, a long-suffering diabetic, then flippantly asked Linda: "Are you familiar with diabetes?"

Of course not, Mom. Linda only had 11 years of college, med school and residency. I'm sure that disease probably slipped right by her. Linda smiled, and I knew then if she could handle my mother, she could live with me.

I can count at least a dozen times I would be sitting in some press box in Dallas or Jacksonville or New Orleans when some stern-looking official would tap me on the shoulder and say there was an emergency phone call from Memphis.

Each time it happened, my heart would begin to race and I would think the worst. After gulping and saying hello, I would hear my mother on the other end of the phone, rattling off something about the game, once asking me at the Cotton Bowl what television station in Memphis would be broadcasting the event.

My mother was both mentor and coach. Early in my career, I called her late one night, barely able to contain my emotion. I breathlessly informed her I had won first place in a sportswriting contest in Alabama.

"Really? That's good," she said dispassionately. "But how tough could that be? Give me a call when you win first place in the country."

The next year, after a series of articles I had written won first place in the nation, I called her with the news.

"Now," she said, "I am impressed."

She was a regular Vince Lombardi when it came to motivation. On January 26, 1983, the newsroom at the *Birmingham Post Herald* was blazing with activity. I was writing the lead story for the paper on the death of Coach Paul "Bear" Bryant, easily the most important of my fledgling career.

My phone kept ringing. But I was under enormous deadline pressure and never stopped hitting the keyboard. Finally, a colleague, tired of the incessant ringing, picked up the phone and interrupted me.

"I hate to bother you," he said, "but your mother is on the line."

I stared a hole in his face.

"She said it was important," he added.

I picked up the phone and grumbled "hello" while I continued typing.

"Are you doing OK?" she asked.

"Yep, and you?" I said hastily.

"Well, I didn't know if you knew or not, but I just saw on Channel 5 that 'Bear' Bryant had died."

To my mother, if it wasn't on local television or in the Memphis paper, it wasn't official.

On weekends such as this, so many memories rush through my mind.

However, when I think of her, I always remember a picture

of Whistler's Mother that hung in our kitchen and the saying right below.

It is a wonderful thing, a mother;
other folks can love you,
but only your mother understands,
She works for you,
looks after you,
loves you,
forgives you anything you may do,
understands you, and then, the
only thing bad she ever does to you,
is to die and leave you."

A BAD QB, OR JUST A LOT OF BAD LUCK?

June 24, 2000

In the pantheon of great and glorious quarterbacks at the University of Alabama -names such as Joe Namath, Kenny Stabler, Bart Starr and Jay Barker- Freddie Kitchens probably would rank (at least, in some people's minds) as the worst who ever wore Crimson.

To most fans, Kitchens wasn't a quarterback – he was a punch line.

Once, when Kitchens was named one of the 19 finalists for the Johnny Unitas Award, a pundit muttered: "Did I miss something or is the Unitas Award given for the quarterback who can eat the most pizzas or throw the most touchdowns?"

When Kitchens got in trouble before his penultimate game at Alabama in 1997 -supposedly for signing autographs at the hotel and missing the team bus- the public roared with incredulity. "C'mon, Freddie," they seemed to be saying, "who in their right mind would believe someone wanted your autograph?"

Another joke made the rounds that Kitchens once had completed 15 consecutive passes in a game - three of them to Alabama players. When the school's home field was under construction for renovation a few years ago, the joke went: The only thing expanding faster than Bryant-Denny Stadium was Kitchens' waistline.

He was called "Fat Freddie" and the "Pillsbury Dough Boy", and he was harassed by the news media, fans and even behind his back by some of his coaches like no Alabama player in history.

Today, the 25-year-old from Attalla looks back at his turbulent Tide experience with a smile, even though the scars have not completely healed.

"It's pretty amazing to be the worst quarterback in Alabama history and end up third on the all-time passing lists," Kitchens said. "It's all about perception."

Perception, as they say, is reality, and these days, Kitchens is employed as a graduate assistant coach under Nick Saban at LSU. Four weeks from today, he will be married, and the reality of the matter is, he never has been happier in his life.

The road since graduation (a degree in public relations, of all things) has been filled with wrong turns and quick stops. With his once-promising career as a baseball pitcher over because of a nagging injury, Kitchens wanted to play in the NFL but could not get a contract. Eventually, he found work in Italy, with the idea of moving to Saskatchewan a few months later with a promise from the Canadian Football League team.

As luck would have it, Kitchens separated his shoulder. End of career.

Kitchens got out the yellow pages calling coaches, and he eventually found a job at Glenville State in West Virginia (for former Auburn assistant Rick Trickett). This winter, Trickett took a job at LSU, and Kitchens went along as a graduate assistant (most of his time is spent working on the skill positions with another former Auburn assistant, Jimbo Fisher).

Interestingly, Kitchens had two other offers from SEC schools. But none from his alma mater.

In 1993, Kitchens arrived in Tuscaloosa with high hopes and bulging expectations.

An Alabama assistant told Gene Stallings, the head coach at the time, that he had Kitchens ranked ahead of Peyton Manning (this is NOT a misprint) on their charts among high school prospects.

Washington State Coach Mike Price wanted the gunslinger from Etowah High School to replace Drew Bledsoe. Price told Kitchens there were nine quarterbacks on the school's recruiting list, and he was No. 1.

After Kitchens signed with Alabama, Ryan Leaf took his place at Washington State. (In case you have forgotten, Manning and Leaf were the first two players selected in the 1998 NFL draft).

Could Kitchens have kept that kind of company had he gone somewhere other than Alabama? He is quiet for a moment. However, in the sounds of silence, the answer seems evident.

If there was one incident that probably haunted Kitchens' career at Alabama, it came shortly before the 1995 season. The same week the punishing NCAA sanctions came down, Kitchens made the news for being involved in an altercation at a Jacksonville nightclub. The reports said Kitchens, along with a friend, were charged with public intoxication and pinching a young lady on the derriere.

Kitchens professes his innocence to this day (contrary to news media reports at the time, the friend was the one accused of the rump pinching). Kitchens paid a fine, and the case was dropped.

In the public's eye, he paid a much bigger price. Kitchens never was forgiven, and the case never was forgotten.

Not long afterward, in a critical series at Legion Field, with the Tide trailing late against Southern Miss, Kitchens went to the line of scrimmage, barking out the cadence.

"I was looking around as I was calling the numbers and the linebacker from Southern Miss screamed over at me, 'Hey, Freddie, you want to have a beer after the game?'"

The other big issue was his weight.

"Alabama recruited me at 232 pounds and throughout my entire career, my weight was 230 to 235," Kitchens said.

Kitchens' career at Alabama came down to one game. As quarterback of what many people described as the worst Crimson Tide team in 40 years, Alabama, 4-6 at the time, went to Auburn in 1997 with a chance for salvation.

"I had started 27 straight games and got pulled for my last one at Alabama (as well as the one the week earlier against Mississippi State)," Kitchens said, because of the infamous autograph incident.

Hardly anyone believed Alabama could win the game with Lance Tucker at quarterback. And they were right.

Kitchens came into the game in relief and turned in one of the gutsiest performances in Alabama history. It appeared Kitchens' final evening in Crimson would be his finest hour. The game at Jordan Hare Stadium seemingly was won. Alabama had the ball. Then came the ill-fated swing pass from Kitchens to Ed Scissum.

In the midst of the wee hours of the morning, taking the jarringly quiet bus ride back to Tuscaloosa, Kitchens started crying, and the tears would not stop.

"I just couldn't believe how it all ended," Kitchens said of the shattering, last-second 18-17 loss to Auburn.

Time has passed and today, Kitchens is content coaching in Baton Rouge, LA.

Kitchens said he has not thought much about the Nov. 4 game against the Crimson Tide at Tiger Stadium.

However, late at night, Kitchens still thinks about Alabama in a different light.

"After being a fan for 18 years, it's still my school," Kitchens said. "I think about going back there to coach all the time. That is my dream."

Here's hoping that dream comes true one day for Freddie Kitchens, a good kid who has suffered enough bad luck in his life.

ANDY'S NO DANDY AS PRESIDENT

July 7, 2000

This should be a wonderful time for the University of Alabama family. After several tumultuous years -where screaming headlines about the NCAA woes and the Mike DuBose controversy took center stage- all is quiet now on the western front.

There is a level of enthusiasm and excitement about the school's football program that hasn't been felt in many years. National publications have Alabama ranked high in the nation's top five (*The Sporting News* has the Crimson Tide at No. 3) and some pundits have picked the Tide to go all the way.

However, despite the clear blue skies on the horizon, there remains a single dark and sinister cloud hovering over the Crimson Empire. His name is Andrew Sorensen. Unfortunately, he runs the university.

President Sorensen is pompous, condescending, supercilious, impervious, brusque and capricious. And these are his good points.

Sorensen constantly talks down to reporters, coaches (and their wives) and administrative people as if he is king and they are his subjects. The man is an embarrassment and most reasonable people associated both inside and out of the university recognize this point.

Unfortunately, the only people who have been blinded by his ways are the people who inexplicably hired him: members of the university's board of trustees.

I've always thought it fatuous for people to start calling for the firing of a university president simply because of his attitudes or actions on athletics. The school is bigger than the football program (at least, that is the rumor). Even though Joab Thomas hired Bill Curry -easily, the most imbecilic coaching appointment in modern history- I thought he was an excellent president.

Still, Sorensen's approach and attitude toward running the school, including athletics, finally has reached the point where most sensible people believe he should go. It isn't one thing he has done in four years at the helm. It is everything.

This week, Sorensen made two separate statements about the athletic department. Taken literally, the comments don't mean a lot. But when you read between the lines, many fans and alumni were left shaking their heads in disbelief.

First, the story about the football staff receiving a scrawny pay raise.

"There's been a lot of misinformation out there," Sorensen said. "I don't know how all this rumor starts that I'm opposed to pay raises for the assistant coaches. It is simply not true."

Of course, it was true, since Sorensen has held staff at bay since the end of a championship season. Ask any coach privately.

On the subject of the Million Dollar Band going to the Rose Bowl for the UCLA game, Sorensen again responded with emblematic nicenellyism.

"I think if boosters are as supportive of the athletic department as they say they are," Sorensen said, "that it makes sense to let the athletic director -whom they told me was the best choice (to hire) I could possibly make in the entire world- (make the decision)."

In other words, don't blame me. That's Mal Moore's decision.

Finebaum Said...

What a crock! And what an affront to Moore, a genuinely nice man still learning the ropes, to treat him with such rawness.

Of course, Sorensen is still ticked off because he didn't get his way on the Moore hiring. It is no secret Sorensen pursued Florida State Athletic Director Dave Hart, the highly respected Alabama graduate.

Twice, in 1996 when he hired one of the biggest boobs in history (Bob Bockrath) and again last year, Sorensen desperately wooed Hart. Friends of Hart said he privately told them he would have loved to have returned to his alma mater, but he would not work for Sorensen.

The bottom line: Sorensen thinks Moore -and nearly everyone else who is not up to his intellectual level- is a rube and a redneck. Naturally, he views Alabama football fans in the same light. Trust me on this one.

This is a man who tried to run Gene Stallings out of town from the moment he stepped foot in the Rose Administration building. This is a man who favors bow ties (that should tell all you need to know) and was too good to show up for the press conference announcing Mike DuBose's promotion to head coach in 1996.

Of course, Sorensen's gargantuan ego couldn't allow him to totally miss the festivities. He had to address the news conference by speakerphone live from New York, where he was probably getting a charisma bypass.

Two years later, Sorensen apparently went loco over DuBose's coaching at the disastrous Arkansas loss, leaving Cecil Hurt, the lowkey, but highly respected sports editor of *The Tuscaloosa News*, to write, "His absence from the press conference announcing DuBose is still one of the most transparent and childish acts I've witnessed, although those who were within earshot say his tirade at the Arkansas game was a close second."

Whether one agreed or disagreed with Sorensen's decision to retain DuBose last August, nobody could believe his statements shortly afterward, when Sorensen said he did not know "for sure" if he can still trust DuBose to abide by NCAA regulations.

"That does make it difficult," Sorensen said.

That is one of the most outrageous statements I've read in a career of covering college athletics.

A week later, this charlatan showed up at practice, with his arm around DuBose (does he remind you just a little bit of Bill Clinton?) and gave a pep talk to the team, leaving many people to question, "Haven't these young men suffered enough?"

In the midst of all this, he seemed to be spending more time at the campus Kinko's having his resume polished than running the school. He campaigned for the top position at Vanderbilt, even calling people in this state asking for help to get the job.

When Vanderbilt prudently looked the other way, Sorensen set his sights on the University of North Carolina. Fittingly, they rejected his overtures, too.

However, the most astonishing rebuke came from the University of Florida, where Sorensen had held the No. 2 position of provost and chief academic officer for seven years.

William Muse, the Auburn president who wasn't even looking for work, made Florida's short list while Sorensen -left out of the search- probably panted like a junkyard dog at feeding time.

Danny Sheridan, the sports analyst for *USA Today* and a University of Alabama graduate, recently told a Bar Association meeting in Mobile:

"When Sorensen was hired, I called a member of the Florida Board of Regents to find out about him. He said succinctly: 'We owe Alabama big time for taking that elitist wannabe off our hands.'"

Alabama defeated Florida twice on the football field last year. However, it appears the Gators might have had the last laugh. They are rid of this man while Alabama is stuck with him.

Don't you think it's about time Alabama did away with him as well?

NASCAR DYING A FAST DEATH

July 10, 2000

In the past decade, the fastest growing sport in America has been NASCAR. With dazzling marketing, the sport finally shed the image of being backwoods and redneck.

With slick stars such as Jeff Gordon and Tony Stewart, the sport became middle-of-the- road and Madison Avenue -as well as Main Street- fell in love.

However, that could change in the coming days.

With the second fatal crash in a matter of months, the same fans that rushed to the fast tracks with pockets full of money might head to some other venue, where the price of fame and fortune might not be so high.

Jim Murray, the late sportswriter with the Los Angeles Times, once caught unmitigated grief when he began a column about the Indy 500, writing: "Gentleman, start your coffins!"

Unfortunately, the same line might be applicable today to NASCAR.

People go to the races for myriad reasons - even the crashes. Just like people go to hockey games for the fights.

However, even the sickest puppy on the block doesn't want to see someone killed.

Yet, these days, that has become common at speedways -particularly in New England- and I think fans will eventually look the other way and find somewhere else to spend their money.

NASCAR officials talk a good game about everything, from racial relations to track safety. However, their pathetically predictable statements, every time some rising star goes from pit road to a body bag, will not be enough. It won't be enough until someone does something about the problems ... and fast.

It won't be enough until NASCAR sends a message they

really care rather than offering lip service. Oh, well, another death seems to be the message from NASCAR. But fellows, the show must go on.

These days in NASCAR, they have the act down to a science. A driver dies. The track personnel huddle and officials show grief. Then, the practice runs continue.

Has anyone ever considered calling off a race in deference to the dead? Of course, not. Don't want to upset those sponsors and those fans or the stock price on Wall Street, now, do they?

And nobody is outraged when it happens.

The cameras zoom in some big-bellied bubba with a wad of Red-Man in the corner of his mouth while proudly showing off his three green teeth, and he says: "Mighty bad what happened, isn't it. But, ya, know, that's racin'."

When a boxer dies in the ring, the nation screams bloody murder. There are congressional hearings. When a race car driver perishes, everybody covers for people that own the track or the France family or both.

It is okay for Congress to worry about gambling on college basketball. But it doesn't seem to concern them when young men are dying on our tracks.

Is the France family so powerful they have everyone in their back pocket?

"Well, it's not just a show," said Mike Helton, NASCAR's senior vice-president. "NASCAR is more like a community and if a citizen of the community passes away, the community still has to go on. Your heart's not in it 100 percent but (the race) has to go on."

It has to go on?

After two deaths in practically the same place, I wouldn't race a bicycle at this speedway. But then again, NASCAR knows best. I just hope the France family can sleep at night.

Their marketing brilliance have made millionaires out of many young drivers and car owners, to say nothing of the France Family Trust. They have transformed a hillbilly sport into one of the great American success stories.

The drivers know the risk. Sure, we've all heard that before. But the lack of care or compassion from the group that runs NASCAR makes me ill. It is nauseating. Just once, perhaps, the moguls of NASCAR will think about something other than greed.

Perhaps, once, after their monotonous moments of silence and sorrowful statements, they will stand up in front of the cameras and say: "You know, we just need to take a break this weekend. We've talked to the television networks and our sponsors and it's jut not right to continue racing."

But, of course, this will never happen. To the France family and those who work at NASCAR, the mantra is passing the buck in order to make more money.

Too bad about Kenny Irwin and Adam Petty. But there's always a young driver waiting in the wings, willing to take the necessary risk.

Even if it kills them.

FAITH LIFTS DUBOSES THROUGH SCANDAL

July 22, 2000

They sat together, holding hands and giggling and eyeing each other like teenagers in love. They joked about a football play she once gave him for the Iron Bowl.

He chuckled, and said: "Oh, yeah, it was the screen pass (in 1997 that Ed Scissum fumbled, costing the Tide a sure victory at Jordan-Hare Stadium) against Auburn."

Everyone laughed.

Everyone smiled.

Finebaum Said...

To steal one of the oldest cliches in journalism: What a difference a year makes.

Last summer, Polly and Mike DuBose were facing the most searing crisis of their lives. At this juncture in 1999, we were still a few days away from the public revelation that the coach had misled the University of Alabama administration about an inappropriate relationship with his secretary.

When the news was dropped on the public like a nuclear bomb -and the ensuing conflagration- even DuBose's few remaining supporters conceded only a miracle could save his career. Call it whatever you choose, but an amalgamation of events occurred, from the Louisiana Tech loss to the firing of Athletic Director Bob Bockrath to a twist of fate in Gainesville, FL, and the ultimate Southeastern Conference championship.

Today, the Tide is high, ranked among the favorites for the national championship and the sure pick to win the league title next week when the swarm of news media members arrives for the SEC Media Days.

And the DuBoses -married now just days short of 25 years- have never seemed happier. They talked dreamily about the few days they recently stole at a small cabin by a remote lake, just the two of them. She smiled at him with doe eyes. He smiled back at her with a wink.

How did this happen? How did their marriage survive innumerable jokes and incessant mockery? How did it survive mistrust and deception?

Both Polly and Mike DuBose have the same answer: faith. The two have appeared in myriad churches over the state in recent months, sharing their testimony as well as their anguish. It is both a poignant and compelling story, one with a spectacularly happy ending.

Naturally, there are detractors and skeptics. But neither Mike nor Polly have time to focus on the negative. Neither really cares to.

Mike DuBose spends time every morning reading and studying the Bible. He readily admits his mistakes, both in his personal life as well as his professional career.

"I wasn't ready to be the head coach at Alabama," DuBose said recently. "I just wasn't prepared."

DuBose said he became caught up in the hype and hubbub of the position and the rarefied air in which the head coach at the University of Alabama travels. He became intoxicated with the power and the trappings. The 47-year-old coach concedes what happened last year easily was the most difficult thing in his life. However, both DuBose and his wife quickly will say it also was the best year of their lives.

Naturally, this raises eyebrows, but DuBose explained he was at the end of the rope, "headed down a one-way street of death and eternal life in hell. ... I had to change and accept Jesus Christ as my Savior."

Clearly, DuBose is a changed man this summer as he prepares for the most anticipated Alabama football season in recent memory. Having watched him up close several times in recent months, playing 18 holes of golf, sitting in the church pew listening to his testimony and interviewing him for this story, I clearly have seen a man at peace with himself and the milieu that surrounds him.

When the subject turned to a recent NCAA probe and the allegations that Florida Coach Steve Spurrier personally turned in Alabama to authorities, DuBose smiled and circumspectly chose his words.

"I respect Steve as both a coach and a man," DuBose said.

DuBose lavished praise on Logan Young, the controversial Memphis millionaire and close friend of the late Paul "Bear" Bryant. University of Tennessee football fans repeatedly have accused Young of getting too close to the Memphis recruiting scene, which Alabama has subjugated in recent years. Young repeatedly has denied any wrongdoing.

DuBose said he considers Young "a personal friend" and said

he isn't concerned about the allegations, saying the charges against Alabama were only "alleged" and the school had not heard anything officially from the authorities.

DuBose said he welcomes high rankings in the polls and joked "a couple of years ago, everyone was praising us and trying to schedule us for homecoming."

Not anymore. These days, Alabama is public enemy No. 1. However, DuBose seems to be enjoying the moment. Alabama is back. His career has been saved. But most important, his family and faith have been restored.

COTTRELL STAYS CALM AS RUMORS SWIRL

August 5, 2000

In the wake of a second suspension of Alabama's renowned recruiting coordinator for minor rules violations in less than a year, some insiders in Tuscaloosa privately are asking: How many more lives does Ronnie Cottrell have?

The late summer breezes are full of whispers in the woods about questions the NCAA seems to be asking and even some die-hard Alabama supporters are growing increasingly nervous that another shoe could be about to drop.

One common thread in the rumors concerns the 41-year-old Cottrell, who came to Alabama three years ago from Florida State and has a reputation as the finest recruiter in college football.

"I think criticism is something you have to accept," Cottrell said this week when asked about the daily batch of rumors. "I try to worry about things I can control. I can't worry about what someone at Georgia, Tennessee or Mississippi say about Ronnie

Cottrell. I'm not going to judge those people.

"It says in the Bible in Matthew 7:1, 'Do not judge or you too will be judged.'"

Four weeks from today, Alabama opens the season on national television in the Rose Bowl against UCLA. Yet, in addition to the talk about the bountiful harvest of freshmen reporting this weekend and public debate over quarterbacks Andrew Zow and Tyler Watts, rumors continue to fly from various quarters (namely, Knoxville, Gainesville, FL, and Auburn) about the NCAA.

Are these people floating nasty and vicious rumors as a means of getting back at Alabama -in other words, sour grapes- because of dominance on the recruiting trails? Or is there really something out there that has caught the eyes of the reviled NCAA?

"I've heard all this stuff for 10 years," Cottrell said. "At FSU, the same rumors were out there. Certainly, I don't think there is any truth to them."

Cottrell said if some rival coaches have information on Alabama, they should send the charges to the proper authorities, such as the Southeastern Conference or NCAA office. Florida Coach Steve Spurrier concedes he has done just that. Whether others have done the same is unclear.

Currently, though, there is enough smoke in the proverbial SEC forest to alert Smokey the Bear.

"I know of nothing that I should be concerned about, but all of this just seems to continue," Cottrell said. "I am uncomfortable with all of this.

"I just know this program will do what's right."

Cottrell is believed to be close to Logan Young, the Memphis millionaire who was in former Alabama Coach Paul "Bear" Bryant's inner circle. Rivals schools repeatedly have accused Young of getting too close to the Memphis recruiting scene, which Alabama has dominated in recent years. Young has denied any wrongdoing.

Two weeks ago, Alabama Coach Mike DuBose said he considered Young "a personal friend" and conceded he wasn't concerned about the allegations, saying the charges against Alabama were only "alleged" and the school had not heard anything officially from the authorities.

Some people also have found comments DuBose made recently in *The Commercial Appeal* in Memphis mildly curious, on the subject of Cottrell's overall coaching ability.

"Ronnie is going to get a big-time head coaching job," DuBose said. "What gets overlooked is he's a great on-the-field coach with our tight ends and kickers."

Some people wondered if DuBose wasn't trying to promote Cottrell in the likely event the University of Memphis makes a coaching change at the end of this season.

Meanwhile, Cottrell simply shakes his head while trying to dodge the daily blitz of bullets.

"It's ironic we're approaching one of the most exciting seasons in our program's history and this stuff continues," Cottrell said. "My job is to coach football, and I'm going to do that until my job changes."

The timing of the public revelation Thursday that Cottrell sold four tickets to the Orange Bowl to a family friend of a player will only feed the frenzy. However, despite Athletic Director Mal Moore saying the discipline (keeping Cottrell off the road during the May evaluation period) was related only to this specific case, some skeptics think the school might have been taking a preemptive strike against Cottrell in order to protect itself down the road if more serious revelations come out.

"We self-report things all the time," Cottrell said. "That is part of compliance. Things happen and we turn it in."

If Cottrell can swim successfully out of the shark-infested waters, one would think his coaching career looms bright. Last year, he was mentioned for several head coaching positions. If the Tide has another banner year, Cottrell's stock will rise, considering he had three recruiting classes at FSU ranked No. 1 in news media surveys and two others ranked No. 2.

All of his recruiting classes at Alabama have been sensational. Still, Cottrell admits the allegations and incessant speculation have stung. Whether the pain is only skin deep or does permanent damage to his career remains to be seen.

"It hurts your feelings," Cottrell said. "This is a tough game. Hopefully, I'm in God's will doing what I'm supposed to be doing. I turn to faith and turn the problems that I have to Him. I know what the truth is. That's all I can do."

CRIMSON TIDE'S RISE TO TOP GOES BY BOOK

August 12, 2000

Please don't consider the following message too pushy, but there is no time like the present.

I am here today for the singular purpose of plugging a book. My book. So pardon me if I get right to the point. By ordering early (and often), you can receive a nice discount and perhaps even get the coffee table, leather-bound edition (it will be signed and numbered) in time for the holidays.

This is not a sales pitch, but I wouldn't make the same mistake that many folks made in January 1993. Do you remember how people were caught completely by surprise? Do you remember those long lines of pushy fans (like a WWF crowd) in the bitter January cold outside bookstores trying to get those *Sports Illustrated* commemorative issues? Remember the fear and loathing in the Crimson Empire?

As George W. Bush's poppy likes to say: "Not this time. Won't happen. Promise you that."

My book, which I hope soon becomes your book, is entitled, "Lucky No. 13: The Extraordinary Story of Alabama's 2000 National Championship Season."

I've already sold it to a big New York publisher. In order to get the book (hard bound, $49.95, and leather-bound, $299.95) under your tree for Christmas, we will have to print right after Alabama defeats Florida 45-0 (imagine the look on Spurrier's face when he loses for a third consecutive time to Mike DuBose!) in the Southeastern Conference championship game and before the Tide squashes Nebraska 77-0 in the national championship game in the Orange Bowl. But who cares?

Why let the facts get in the way of becoming a millionaire? Finally, don't delay; call today (1-800-RollTideRoll) while supplies last. As an added bonus, we also will throw in, free of charge, Ronnie Cottrell's latest book, "101 NCAA Rules I Just Didn't Know."

We now return you to regular programming. ...

Would somebody puh-leeze tell me what's going on here? Would someone explain how Alabama went from the outhouse last September (remember the Louisiana Tech game?) to the penthouse of college football?

What's so amazing is that Alabama fans -usually the most optimistic (please note I did NOT use the phrase arrogant) group in the land- are underestimating the Tide, at least in comparison to the national news media.

Most fans in Alabama think the Tide will roll this season. However, even the most zealous supporter sees a loss somewhere along the road to Miami. However, the national news media is out of control. The group, which usually shuns the Tide, has Alabama ranked No. 3 in the AP poll, the USA *Today*/ESPN coaches' poll and the CNN-*SI* poll.

The college football editor for USA *Today's* Internet site this week boldly predicted Alabama would win the national championship. Tim Brando of CBS Sports mouthed the same thing. On another Internet site, a make-believe national championship play-off was held, and the Tide defeated Florida State for the crown.

You literally can't buy a ticket to the games (thousands this week got polite rejections along with refunds), leaving DuBose to start campaigning already for expansion of the stadium. This is a coach with a 21-15 record, and he is talking like Paul W. Bryant after his third national championship.

I missed the glory days of Bryant, although I caught his final act. But can anyone remember enthusiasm and excitement being this high for the Tide?

Back then, Alabama fans were grumpy when they weren't picked No. 1. Now, there is dancing in the streets to be picked in the top five. But how long will Tide fans tolerate DuBose's team being picked No. 3 instead of No. 1?

I don't want to rain on the parade. I don't want to be the lone voice of reason in the wilderness. Although I think this team is loaded with talent and certainly has a chance to compete for the national championship, I'm just really not seeing the same thing that some of my brethren are seeing.

Not to sound like a broken record, but I think it will be extremely difficult to replace the enormous talent of tackle Chris Samuels and running back Shaun Alexander as well as their leadership. I think the confusion over the starting quarterback job has a chance to disrupt the flow of this team. I also believe last year was like a comet in some respects, something that was bright and beautiful and breathtaking, but you don't see one come along often.

In 1999, half of the Tide's games went down to the wire, and seemingly everything went Alabama's way, that is, after the Louisiana Tech disaster and excluding the missed point-after-touchdown kick against Michigan (by then, the season already was a smash).

The staff was in dire straights, and somehow, some way, the strife brought everyone together to work on the same page with a universal and burning goal: to save their jobs.

So the curtain is about to rise on the 2000 season. If everything goes according to plan, it could be one of the finest in Alabama history. But what if doesn't? What if the wheels come off?

Well, I could always change the title of my best-selling book to "Armageddon: How Alabama's bid for a 13th National Championship Got Derailed."

That's the bad news.

The good news is the book will be a lot cheaper and easier to find.

REBELS FANS SHOULD SHUT UP, ALREADY

September 8, 2000

Only in Mississippi could a school, which hasn't been No. 1 in anything but having the most drunk fans at a football game in the past 40 years, raise a ruckus about their best coach since Johnny Vaught leaving town for Auburn. And not shut up about it for two years.

What a joke!

Of course, we are talking about the University of Mississippi.

Before you Ole Miss fans start writing missives (please, don't spill any Dickel on the letters like the last time when I lowered myself to opine about your ilk), I know a little something about this fine football school.

The first college football game I ever went to as a young toddler was at the Liberty Bowl when Memphis State upset Ole Miss. I learned words that night from the inebriated, malodorous, repellent Ole Miss fans I had never heard before in my young days of watching "Batman," "Gilligan's Island" and "Andy Griffith."

It was a big deal for Memphis to beat Ole Miss, since it had never happened before. Of course, that was back in a time when Ole Miss football was something more than a punch line. It was several years removed from a national championship and the Rebels hadn't quite permanently moved into second-class status behind Alabama and Tennessee.

Through the years, Ole Miss excelled at two things in particular: breaking NCAA rules and firing coaches. Finally, the school made a smart coaching hire, bringing Tommy Tuberville on board in 1995 and the Rebels finally were able to see some light at the end of the long and tenebrous tunnel.

All Tub did was restore order to the asylum. He raised a sinking ship, put the shattered pieces back together again (after all, he replaced a coach on a full-time basis whose nickname was "Dog"), and got the NCAA stench out of the uniforms. Tub even tried to do something about the Confederate flag.

Then he made a serious mistake.

He lied.

Instead of being honest (yes, I am talking to Auburn behind the scenes and probably will take the job, because it is a big-time program vs. the minor leagues, since they draw 85,000 to Ole Miss' 45,000 and are offering me approximately $400,000 more per year in salary), he fibbed.

Why did he lie?

Truthfully, he was trying to save the Ole Miss season for the players. Tuberville actually cared about the players he had recruited (the same ones who probably will beat his Auburn team Saturday). They had been through a tough time, and with a 6-2 record, Tuberville assumed the Rebels could win one or maybe even two of the remaining three games against Arkansas, Georgia and Mississippi State. Tub made a serious miscalculation. The Rebels were smashed in the three games, and he was labeled "Benedict Arnold."

Before anyone starts accusing me of condoning lying, let me stop right here for a moment. I am not saying he did the right thing. Tuberville could have been nebulous. He could have given a lot of typical coach-like answers.

There was another issue going on as well.

Bill Oliver was the interim head coach at Auburn and had a lot of support. Tub knew (or at least was told by key Auburn people) if he triggered too much speculation he had the job, there would be upheaval at Auburn in terms of people pushing for Oliver to get the position.

So Tub set out to tell a little white lie and ended up sounding like Bill Clinton talking about sex. He got carried away with his own fiction. He made the proverbial mountain out of a molehill, and one hardly can blame Ole Miss fans for being unhappy.

But get over it.

If Ole Miss people are so happy he's gone, give Tub a big cheer when he comes back Saturday evening. Raise the roof off of creaky little Vaught-Hemingway Stadium. Put the whiskey bottles down (remember the flung bottle in 1993 aimed at the Alabama sideline?). Tone down the off-color cheers. Show some class for the first time in Ole Miss history.

Of course, it won't happen.

Somehow, class and Ole Miss fans don't mix very well in the same sentence. It would be a sight to see, though. Ole Miss fans giving credit to Tommy Tuberville - the man who saved their stinking little football program.

DUBOSE SPURS LOSS
OF WORDS ... ALMOST

October 30, 2000

Sports columnists are not supposed to run out of words. Ever. We are paid to pontificate about any and all subjects, regardless of the situation.

However, I must admit up front that Mike DuBose really is trying my patience. In four years of describing his tenure at the University of Alabama, my ink well has run dry. What else can be said that hasn't already been written?

I have searched volumes of dictionaries and bought a new thesaurus. I'm still struggling to find the words. On second thought, I'm not struggling at all. I've given up.

In the first year alone, I used up five year's worth of adjectives trying to describe the losses against Kentucky and Louisiana Tech. The debacle at Auburn practically finished me off. After all, how do you depict a play so stupid to blow the biggest game of the year? What was DuBose's excuse? Since he wasn't wearing a headset, DuBose conceded he didn't know the call.

With most coaches, one would have smelled a rat. Not DuBose. One look at him after the game convinced me he was telling the truth. He should have been fired on the spot. But Alabama fans gave him a free pass. Big mistake.

In year two, DuBose took a top 25 squad to Arkansas and lost 42-6. Words were hard to find after that one. After watching the season-ending 38-7 loss to Virginia Tech in the Music City Bowl, I remembered sitting over my laptop in the press box, shaking my head, desperate for a different way of describing an Alabama loss.

DuBose shocked us again the following year, even before the season began, admitting he had lied about an affair with his secretary. I didn't hold back that day, firing away at my computer, saying, "Give him the boot!"

Of course, cooler heads prevailed at the Capstone. DuBose survived. Big mistake.

When the team lost to Louisiana Tech (again), the executioner was called. Yet, before the guns were aimed and fired, Alabama had upset Florida and DuBose's career was back on track.

This year, we in the media tried a different route. Everyone in the nation (remember Tim Brando picking the Tide to win the national championship and Danny Sheridan pleading for DuBose's job last year and tabbing the Tide to go 10-1 this time around?), felt this was the shining moment.

We all know about this year. It's one thing to write about losing to UCLA, Southern Miss, Arkansas and Tennessee.

But Central Florida?

No way. There is no such thing in a sports writing class that prepares someone covering the University of Alabama to know what to say about something like this.

Where do you begin and where do you end? Do you state the obvious (DuBose should have been relieved of duty immediately) or do you write something stupid (he will be evaluated at the end of the season)?

Do you praise Coach DuBose for all of the fine things he has done at Alabama (could I possibly get back to you on that?) or do you continue to dredge up all of the negatives (see above)?

Do you immediately go over to Mal Moore and interview him after the game? No, Mal learned under the Bear that when it doubt, just mumble something indecipherable.

Or does one simply take a deep breath, and just count the days until this pathetic regime finally comes to an end?

The bottom line: There are better days ahead for Tide fans. This season will eventually cease and Alabama will have a new coach.

Until then, the blame game will rage on. There are three games remaining. Yes, Alabama can win all three and make the SEC championship game against Florida. Wouldn't that be interesting? If Central Florida could score 40 on Alabama's permeable defense, what do you think the University of Florida would put on the board?

Well, of course, that is not going to happen.

Saying Alabama has a mathematical chance of winning the SEC West is no different than saying Ralph Nader has a chance of getting 270 electoral votes and being the next President of the United States. His only chance is being on the ballot just like the Tide's only chance is the fact it still has three games left.

This program isn't going to win any championship. It might win a game or two. But there are so many splinters, so many problems - this bunch will be lucky to get on the right plane Friday for the trip to Baton Rouge, La.

This program is like a bad marriage simply waiting for the final divorce decree to come through. DuBose is still the head coach, but he is clearly separated from the program. Everyone can talk a good game. But it's over and has been since the Southern Miss loss.

Now, would someone please just make it official and put everyone -especially those of us paid to describe the action- out of our misery?

Finebaum Said...

NOTE TO NCAA: BE GENTLE WITH TIDE

November 27, 2000

NCAA Enforcement Staff C/O University of Alabama Athletic Department, Tuscaloosa, AL 35487

To whom it may concern:

Welcome back, guys. It's been a while since you folks last visited and I wanted to make sure you knew the lay of the land.

We hope you enjoy the visit and don't forget, if you go to Dreamland, it's all you can eat and don't worry about the bill. I've talked to some of my big-time 'Bama buddies and we're going to take care of anything you boys need.

I know during your last visit in 1995, you weren't treated very well. There were rumors about conflicts with Hootie Ingram and Gene Stallings. Those fellows are gone.

We are not nearly as haughty as we were back then. After all, the Tide was fresh off a national championship and we were, after all, still regarded as a sacred cow.

Some other things have changed as well.

Remember how Alabama used to look down its nose at Auburn when the school got investigated every three or four years for rules violations? Remember the battle cry when Auburn celebrated its centennial a few years back? "Auburn football: 100 years of cheating."

Alabama owned Auburn in every category. We had 12 national championships to their measly one, and even that one had an asterisk because the school was in NCAA jail.

Alabama had never been hit by the NCAA and it was wonderful.

However, the probation in 1995, combined with two losing

200

seasons, has really opened our eyes.

Now, I know you guys are going to interview a number of assistant coaches and players about some of these allegations. However, please, take some time to go by the coach's office and review film of this year. Please look at the Southern Miss game, the Central Florida game and the finale against Auburn. Now, I know you gentlemen are investigators and not football coaches. But please, after reviewing those games, I want to know if you saw a single player in Crimson worth paying for. Now, c'mon, be serious. If Alabama paid for any of these guys, the coaches should be filing suit for fraud.

Now, we know the real reason you guys are here. Phil Fulmer has been running his fat yap for so long about all of those players in Memphis going to Alabama, you guys just had to investigate. What does Tennessee have on the NCAA? Every four or five years, there is a big investigative story about the Vols doing something wrong. The NCAA sends investigators up there to Rocky Top. The next thing you know, the NCAA is practically sending UT an apology letter for having wasted their time. Never seen anything like it in my life. UT has a professor screaming bloody murder about academic fraud and you guys go up there and talk to Eric Locke and his daddy about Alabama.

Meanwhile, Doug Dickey and Fulmer slap each other on the back, head down to Krispy Kreme to pick up a dozen for breakfast and decide to add 10,000 more seats to an already bulging Neyland Stadium.

Now, I don't want to sound like Al Gore (another Tennessee product) here and screech and beg, but hasn't Alabama suffered enough? I mean, this program has been ridiculed and humiliated by the NCAA. This program has lost to Louisiana Tech, Southern Miss, Central Florida. This program had its 30-year winning streak snapped at Tiger Stadium. This program now loses on a regular basis to second-tier schools like Arkansas and Mississippi State.

Finebaum Said...

Auburn comes into our house and puts an old-fashioned, bare-knuckle, country whipping on us. We can't even score on the visitors from the Cow College.

We are in the process of a coaching search and you guys drop this bombshell.

Couldn't you at least waited a few weeks? You had to announce this right when we were going outside the family and hiring a great coach like Butch Davis. Well, need I say more? Please go easy on us. Please don't make things any worse.

Isn't it bad enough that Alabama is the only school from the SEC West who isn't bowl-eligible and one of only three along with Vanderbilt and Kentucky in the conference?

I won't beg any more. I won't say anything else. We promised in 1995 that we would be better citizens. And when the NCAA exonerated the Tide in 1999 during another probe, your geeky chairman even praised us. Let us only hope the third NCAA probe of Alabama in six years will be the charm.

Finally, we also understand -this can now be revealed for the first time on American soil- as part of the NCAA sanctions in 1995, Alabama had to hire Mike DuBose. I have always wondered why Bob Bockrath went for DuBose over Davis or Frank Beamer. Now, we know that DuBose was forced on Alabama in an effort to prevent the death penalty, although, I'm not sure which one would have been worse.

Sincerely,
Your Pal Paul.

CHAOTIC YEARS BEHIND FANS' TEPID REACTION

December 6, 2000

Perhaps the most telling sign of this week's coaching announcement was the polite but reserved reaction Alabama fans have shown toward the hiring. Now, of course, the Tide family was interested in the selection of Dennis Franchione. But having watched every transition since Paul Bryant's retirement, this one has seemingly registered an unremarkable reading on the Crimson Tide Richter scale.

In some respects, it just goes to show how low this program has fallen over the years.

I think for the most part, fans are pleased with Franchione's hiring. As a matter of fact, outside of a few cynics on the sideline, the response has been optimistic.

Oh, there may be a few feminists stewing over one remark made by Coach Fran at his news conference. Eyebrows were raised when he called his wife, Kim, to the front of the room and said: "If you don't think I can recruit, just check this out." It's not as if Coach Fran had his wife walk down a runway to show off her wares. But people are funny about such things.

Franchione is smooth and silky, but not in an offensive way, such as Bill Curry. He is bold and confident, but not quite arrogant (see Steve Spurrier). Clearly, he is a control freak, but is that really so bad, considering who he is replacing? Mike DuBose was a coach who rarely looked as if he knew who the opponent was on a given Saturday.

At his inauguration ceremony Monday, Franchione paid homage to the Bear. Of course, that is standard fare at the Capstone. I've always wondered if a new coach failed to mention Coach Bryant, would he be shot on sight?

Of course, the school rounded up the usual suspects for the announcement - Gene Stallings, Billy Neighbors, Bart Starr and of course, Lee Roy Jordan, who has secretly pined to run the show for years and is finally getting credit for this hiring, even though he never met the new coach until last week.

Unlike recent hires, there is really nothing in Franchione's resume to find fault with. Unlike Ray Perkins, Curry, Stallings and DuBose, he doesn't bring a losing record as a head coach to the program. He has won everywhere. He has been successful everywhere.

Perkins walked in with a chip on his shoulder. Curry had to fend off criticism he had never beaten Auburn (something that never changed). Stallings had been fired at Texas A&M and Arizona (in the NFL). However, at his news conference, his Bear-like resonance and deportment both inspired and energized the troops, suffering from the synthetic Curry era.

The beginning of the DuBose era was interesting as well. Tide fans acknowledged he was green around the gills. However, they felt DuBose's ability on the recruiting trails would ensure the Tide great success. It was just a matter of time.

With Franchione, there is quiet optimism about the future but certainly not a high degree of confidence. Quite honestly, after the past decade, nobody really knows what to believe or think anymore.

In the 11 seasons since Curry left, Alabama football has seen it all. There was a year with 12 losses (if you go by the NCAA record book). There were two actual losing seasons, 4-7 (in 1997) and 3-8 (2000). Twice, Alabama lost five games (7-5 in 1990 and 7-5 in 1998). Sprinkled in among the mediocre years were two SEC crowns (1992 and 1999) and of course, the national championship.

There was the devastating NCAA probation in 1995 and now, perhaps, more sanctions around the corner. It seems every time Alabama is about to turn the corner, the other shoe drops.

So it is perhaps for these reasons, Alabama fans welcome yet another coach but do so at arm's length.

Of all the tumultuous times of the past years, from Bryant's resignation to Perkins' superciliousness to Curry's botched hiring, there has never been another year like this one.

The high level of arrogance, confidence, optimism (call it whatever you choose) that existed before the 2000 season was unlike anything seen at Alabama since the glory years of Bryant. Bama was back. The rest of the SEC had better just get out of the way.

Now, barely three months later, the program has crashed and burned, the coach has been fired in disgrace, the NCAA is back in town and the school has hired a coach from TCU to rebuild lost fortunes.

And you think the race for president has been crazy.

So with all of these things understood, it is perhaps under-standable why Alabama fans are excited about having a new sher-iff in town. But it's equally understandable why the enthusiasm has been muted.

Franchione will be extended the usual honeymoon period that any Alabama coach is afforded. He should enjoy every moment. Because judging from history, this job of running the Alabama program never gets any easier than the first day.

DALE EARNHARDT

February 24, 2001

It took a death this week to inspire many of us to evaluate what's really important in life.

In passing, perhaps, Dale Earnhardt has left behind some-thing far more important than his seven Winston Cup champi-onships and reputation as the finest NASCAR driver in history.

The news of the tragedy has touched nearly everyone from the president of the United States, the fan in the infield, to the most casual observer.

To watch the reaction, the outpouring of love and the torrents of tears, have soared beyond the best a wordsmith can come up with. For one to say Earnhardt's death transcended sports -the usual cliche we toss out at times like this- is to state the obvious in such a numbing fashion, that it would be an affront to his memory.

It is surprising, however, that so many of us didn't see this coming.

I am not referring to Earnhardt's demise; unfortunately, we have come to expect that in NASCAR with appalling regularity - with its despotic rule and disregard for anything but improving the bottom line. Instead, I am speaking of the reach beyond all boundaries this special man had with so many people in so many places.

Sports Illustrated's cover this week featuring Earnhardt, in black and white, said it all with haunting simplicity. He was a common man who did uncommon things. Earnhardt was a throwback to the '50s and '60s, to a seemingly less complicated time, when neighbors still ran over to one's front yard to celebrate a new Chevy or perhaps, grab a peek inside at a color television set. He was an authentic blue-collar hero, the last, according to race experts, of a dying breed.

Yet, he was also a cash cow for NASCAR in the contemporary era. Last year, souvenir sales for Earnhardt, according to *The Wall Street Journal*, totaled $500 million – approximately 40 percent of all NASCAR revenues.

Through death, Dale Earnhardt has done something I didn't think possible in the often slippery and insalubrious world of sports -polluted with crackheads in the NBA, murderers in the NFL, a collection of spoiled whiners in baseball- to make us remember why so many of us are fans and devotees.

It is easy to say there is no explanation for the trail of tears.

Finebaum Said...

Perhaps, on second thought, there really is.

We see this type of reaction now and then. It pushes our memory deep into the crevasses of another time. For our elders, it might be the death of FDR or JFK that triggers the reaction. Perhaps, for others, it was the passing of Martin Luther King Jr., Elvis Presley or Paul "Bear" Bryant.

To the younger generation, it might be the bone-chilling shock of Challenger exploding on national television or the dreadful death of Princess Diana. Each one invokes a different and piercing memory. Of course, with Earnhardt, more than 200,000 people saw it happen at the speedway and millions more watching at home, making this death in the afternoon even more personal.

For some people, death is the end. You live, you die and you are gone. Often, the death of a celebrity is met with assorted reactions. It forces us to face our mortality. While it is not as painful - for most didn't know Earnhardt other than through television or perhaps, an intermittent trip to Talladega- it still touches a raw nerve. It triggers something within us.

It also raises philosophical questions, namely - the whys of life. We think about our own priorities, and questions such as "Why I am here?", "Why do I do what I am doing?" and "Why do I feel such grief for someone I don't personally know?"

"In a culture which is losing its moral compass, there is growing tendency by some to fill the God-shaped vacuum in our lives with a celebrity who assumes the role of a hero, role model or quasi-deity," says Tom Caradine, the senior associate pastor at Briarwood Presbyterian Church."A reason for this tendency is the media bringing celebrity so close, that we feel we know them personally and some even live their lives vicariously through them. At a celebrity's death, the finite limits of man are exposed and life values built upon a faulty foundation collapses."

Caradine says this kind of pain causes us all to re-evaluate our own lives.

Finebaum Said...

As we think about what is before us, hopefully, the minister says, it challenges us to invest in our families and the lives of others. It might inspire some to accomplish more with their lives, to seek to overcome prejudices, to break down the barrier of the dividing wall between us.

This week may have been the final chapter in the career of NASCAR's greatest driver. Yet, during these long and emotional days, so many of us learned a great deal more about the man behind those dark sunglasses in the No. 3 car... and hopefully so much more about ourselves.

to be continued...